Broken Wings

Broken Wings

A Breathtaking Story of Joy, Hope and Love

Sheree Osborne

Authentic

MILTON KEYNES ● COLORADO SPRINGS ● HYDERABAD

Copyright © 2006 Sheree Osborne

13 12 11 10 09 08 07   8 7 6 5 4 3 2
Reprinted 2007

First published 2006 by Authentic Media
9 Holdom Avenue, Bletchley, Milton Keynes, MK1 1QR, UK
1820 Jet Stream Drive, Colorado Springs, CO 80921, USA
OM Authentic Media, Medchal Road, Jeedimetla Village,
Secunderabad 500 055, A.P., India
www.authenticmedia.co.uk
Authentic Media is a division of IBS-STL U.K., a company
limited by guarantee, with its registered office at Kingstown
Broadway, Carlisle, Cumbria CA3 0HA. Registered in England
& Wales No.1216232. Registered charity 270162

Some of the names in this book have been changed to protect
identities

British Library Cataloguing in Publication Data

A catalogue record for this book is available from the
British Library

ISBN-13 978-1-86024-557-2
ISBN-10 1-86204-557-9

Cover Design by Gerald Rogers
Print Management by Adare Carwin
Printed in Great Britain by J.H. Haynes & Co., Sparkford

Contents

Acknowledgements

There are many people who deserve thanks for the part they have played in my life, and I am most grateful for this opportunity to express those thanks – because without their support, this book would not have been possible.

My first thanks must be to Malcolm Down, for his unwavering faith in me to produce this book. My second thanks are to Sheila Jacobs, my editor, friend and counsel: I thank her for her work in this production.

They say that you can choose your friends but you cannot choose your family, but for me, my friends have become my family. God has given special people to me who have gone the extra mile, and no words can express my heartfelt gratitude towards them. Caroline Prestidge has been my right arm, my trusted confidante and encourager. Without her, I would have buckled many times. To Pauline Vallance: I thank her for her determination in showing me how to hug and be hugged. Diana Bateaux has been my prayer warrior and friend. She has fought many a battle for me in prayer, when I was too weak to fight for myself. To her, I am forever grateful. Then there is Jeff and Brenda Cook, my most faithful friends, whom I truly love; no words can ever properly say how I feel about them. I would also like to thank Dawn Cooper, my friend back in Richmond, who came alongside me in the early days and taught me how to laugh, and with whom I still laugh today. Also, I thank Karen Glassett for her encouragement and friendship which is so invaluable. I thank her for taking the time to read this book, and for the history that we share together. Karen, I treasure every moment that you have been a part of my life.

It is with special thanks that I mention Jeff Scaldwell (who will always be my Pizza Hut King!) and his wife Sylvie. No one could have been given a more beautiful and devoted couple. They have never given up without a fight – even in my darkest hours. Their arms have always been outstretched towards me in an attitude of love and encouragement. They truly are my spiritual parents, whom I ask nothing of but endeavour to imitate as Paul said in Hebrews 6:12.

But my greatest thanks are – and always will be – to Mick, my husband. He is a man of integrity, whose first thought has always been about the needs of others. I love him as much today as I did the night that he faithfully waited outside my house until the early hours of the morning – twenty-seven years ago. He continued to wait for many years for my complete healing and showed more patience than I could ever have dared to hope for.

For many, church has been a place of disappointment and pain. I know, because it was for me, but I pursued it because that is God's heart. His hope is that it will be a place where his loved ones can find rest, love and acceptance; that is my hope too: that you may find a place to rest and find love and people who will go the extra mile with you, as God's healing touch transforms your life . . . and you learn to fly again!

Sheree Osborne
Milton Keynes, December 2005

Dedication

Dedicated to Gerald Richard Osborne
May 1927–December 2004

. . . a father who was a real dad to me, and who I will always love

Chapter 1

Early Days

Have you ever looked at your child and wished they were dead?

Those were the words that screamed out at me from the billboard above the bus station in south Croydon. As the car cruised along, my eyes were transfixed by them. *Have you ever looked at your child . . . and wished they were dead?*

I was on my way to visit friends who were staying in the very town where I had grown up. I was now an adult but still knew the fear that gripped a child whose parent wished them dead; a child who had lived each day of her life with those awful, cruel words resounding in her ears. Those words were pummelled into her, along with the fists of the man with whom she had been left, after her mother had gone. The man was her father, the child was me.

My father was an angry man left with two small children to look after on his own. His words had the ability to cut like a knife and create wounds so deep that by the time I was a teenager, I had no spirit left. I was a mere shell of a human being; everything about me had been

1

destroyed. So I retreated to a dark and sinister place called isolation, and there I stayed through my teenage years, lost and without hope – or so I thought.

My story begins when I was six years of age. Then, I was living with my mother, my father and my brother. I do not remember much about those formative years. They have all but been wiped out by the other thirty that I have lived. I think they were good; I think I was happy. That is, until school began. Up to that point, I had not spent much time away from my mother, but that was all about to change.

'Shireen, come on! It's time for breakfast!' Mum was shouting as I smoothed out imaginary creases on my new yellow gingham dress. I ran downstairs and flung open the breakfast-room door. My brother, Shaun, was sitting in his high-chair, gurgling contentedly.

'You look lovely, Shireen!' Mum smiled, as she put my bowl of cereal in front of me.

I became aware of the funny feeling in my tummy. It was like I had hundreds of tiny little ants walking around inside. My mum said they were called 'butter-flies'.

'I wonder how they got in there? Did they fly in through my mouth whilst I was asleep?' Innocent thoughts ran through my head as I toyed with my cereal.

'Come on, young lady! You don't want to be late for your first day at school, do you?' Mum brought out the hair brush whilst I finished my breakfast.

I hated having my hair brushed because of the length of it. It was jet black – my father was from Pakistan and I had inherited his hair colouring – and went all the way down to my waist. Sometimes I would sit on it. My mother would brush it very gently, trying not to hurt me.

'I wish your father would let me have your hair cut. It would be so much better!' said Mum.

After the hair-brushing session, my mother helped me into my new brown school blazer. It felt heavy and scratchy. Now I was ready to go into the world, unaware that I would have to face it without her.

Mum put my brother in his pushchair and fastened the straps down. He just looked at me with his big brown eyes and gurgled away to himself.

'Bye-bye, Shireen!' My nan appeared at the top of the stairs – she lived in a self-contained flat within the house. 'Have a lovely day, darling!'

I clumsily ran up the stairs and planted a big kiss on her cheek.

'I love you, Nanny!' I watched as she turned and went back into her little kitchen.

After what seemed like a very long journey, that warm and sunny morning, we arrived at my new school. By then, my legs felt heavy and tired.

The concrete playground was full of children. I looked up at my mum.

'They've all got the same clothes on like me, Mummy!' I said, surprised.

'I know. They look smart too, don't they?'

Once again, there they were, my little butterfly friends, come back to play!

A lady approached us. She was built like my nan, with wide hips and a big tummy. She shook my mother's hand and then bent down to my level and said hello; she said she was the head-teacher of the school. Something about her smile failed to impress me. I was getting more and more nervous.

We followed her along white painted corridors, covered with brightly-coloured pictures. There were sinks filled with pots of paint and brushes, and an overpowering smell of powdered paint. I began to feel queasy and in desperation I clung to my mother.

The head-teacher pushed open a door to reveal children sitting on the carpet, again all dressed like me. Little copies all sat in rows. Even their heads spun round at the same time as the door opened.

I grabbed my mother's skirt with such force that the whites of my knuckles were showing. The head-teacher tried to prise my fingers off, but as small as I was, I had a pincer-like grip. Fear turned to terror, then tears welled up in my eyes and I began to cry.

In the end, she managed to loosen my grip, and my mother backed out of the room. The door closed and I was alone. Every pair of eyes was fixed on me. Within moments, it happened. I felt a warm sensation and looked down – I'd wet myself. That was my first day at school!

I soon learnt that the best time of day was when the bell rang at three o'clock. That was the time that I looked forward to the most. I would race to the cloakroom, snatch my shoe-bag off the peg and shoot out into the school playground. Every day I would pick my mother out from the crowd and run towards her with both of my arms outstretched to receive a welcoming hug. I lived for that moment, knowing that the ordeal of another day was over and I could go back to the safety and security of my life: my mother.

But one day, something was different. I searched the crowd of mothers waiting for their children, all smiling with anticipation as they waited for their little ones to run back into the safety of their arms. I began to feel afraid. Where was she? I could not see her. Tears trickled down my cheeks. Then, suddenly, I looked up and there was Nan. What a relief!

'Nanny, where's Mummy? Why isn't she here? Where's Shaun?'

'It's all right, sweetheart. Mummy couldn't come and pick you up because she has a special surprise waiting for you at home and she needs to get it ready for you.' I grabbed my nan's hand. All the way home, I kept wondering what the surprise could be.

When we reached the house, I rushed in. The door to my parents' bedroom was open, and I saw my mother in bed.

'Mummy, where's my surprise?'

She pulled me up beside her and gently kissed me on the cheek.

'There!' She pointed to a blue carrycot at the end of her bed.

I crawled over and peered inside. It was a baby, dressed in white, with tiny little fingers, and a tiny little nose. I gazed in amazement at this living doll.

'Shireen,' said my mother, 'meet your new little sister, Debbie!'

Shaun had his fifth birthday and began attending the same school as me. Now, instead of my brother being in the pushchair when my mother came to pick me up at three o'clock, Debbie was there. And sometimes, my mother didn't come at all; my nan came instead. I didn't mind. I just wanted to get home and play with my new baby sister.

One particular day, Nan picked me up from school. I grabbed her hand, cheerfully. As usual, I just wanted to get home but something seemed wrong. I looked up at her and noticed that her eyes were different; there was a distant expression I hadn't seen before.

'What's wrong, Nanny?' I began to feel fearful. 'Nanny, are Mummy and Debbie all right?' Nan didn't answer me, but held my hand and Shaun's very tightly.

Again and again, I kept asking the same question, but she did not respond. I searched her face for signs of what was wrong, but her face was stony. Nan had never acted like this before; she was always singing and happy. We walked home in absolute silence, and the journey seemed never-ending. As we approached the house, my legs began to feel heavier than they usually did after our long walk. Then, unable to hold on any longer, I wet myself.

'Never mind!' Nan muttered. 'Let's get inside.'

I let go of her hand and raced round the rear of the house, pushing open the back door.

'Mummy, Mummy, we're home!' I ran through the kitchen to the breakfast room, then into the bedroom, but everywhere was empty.

Nanny was right behind me with a stern look on her face.

'Nanny, have I been naughty? Are you angry with me? I don't understand!' I began to cry. 'Nanny, where's Mummy and Debbie? Are they down at the shops?'

Nanny never told me that day that my mother and sister were gone and were not coming back. In silence we ate the sandwiches that she had prepared for us, although we were not hungry. Then, I heard my father's footsteps coming up the stairs. The door flew open and there he stood, tall and menacing. His face was wild with anger. He stared at me with an expression of sheer hatred. Then he began to swear at me.

'You've wet yourself, haven't you, you little . . .? Come here, I'll teach you not to get to the toilet in time, you little . . . !' His huge arms reached out to grab me.

In a flash, Nan came and positioned herself between me and my father. She straightened her back to reach her full height – which was almost a foot shorter than him. She stared straight up into his eyes, showing no fear.

'Don't you *dare* touch her!'

My father stood as still as a statue for a moment and then turned and left the room. I ran to Nan, as did Shaun, and we both clung to her skirt and snivelled. None of us moved until we heard the front door slam.

I was six years of age and my life was just beginning. The world around me should have been a voyage of discovery. I should have been asking about the stars and the moon and why giraffes have such long necks. Instead, I was asking questions about why I was alone.

'Where has my mummy gone? Where's my new sister? Why aren't they here any more?'

But no one ever answered me.

Chapter 2

My Nan

After that day, nothing was the same for me. My mother was no longer there when I got home from school. She was not there to show my childish works of art to, or to listen to my stories. Night after night I curled up in my bed, crying endlessly, desperately trying to think what I had done that was so bad she had to leave. Then worn out and exhausted, sleep would take over and I exchanged one type of darkness for another.

I no longer had a reason to look forward to the three o'clock bell. All the days just seemed the same to me now. I would watch all the other children being swept up in the arms of their mothers, longing to feel that sense of excitement and belonging again. But the happy days when my mother and a gurgling baby greeted me after school, were gone. When I came home, my mother no longer stood over the kitchen sink, washing the dishes. All that I had known was erased in a moment of time. My routine was like a security blanket; with it gone, I was thrown into confusion. Every day I waited in anticipation for something that would never happen; she would never come home again.

Whenever I asked my father the question about my mother coming home, he just kept saying: 'She'll be home soon!'

But day after day, week after week, 'soon' never came!

I loved my nan dearly. She became my world. I knew I was safe when she was around. She had the face of a kindly old lady, her waist and hips were round enough for me to hide behind, and she had the spirit of a warrior to rise up against a man who was built like a boxer. My father might have been twice her stature, but she was totally unfazed by him, even daring to make eye contact, whilst I stood behind her, trembling with fear at his intimidating presence. I came alive when I was with my Nan. It was as if I was able to breathe again. She would sit in her kitchen, with me on her lap, and she would sing songs from *The Sound of Music*. When I came into the house, I no longer ran to the kitchen downstairs to see my mother washing the dishes, now I ran upstairs to see my nan washing *her* dishes. We would laugh together and my brother would be on the floor playing with her kitchen utensils and banging pots and pans, but she never got angry – not with us, anyway. We had picnics and sandwiches on a big rug in the middle of her kitchen when it was grey and cloudy outside.

She tried so hard to keep things as normal as possible for me and my brother. She entertained us with her singing and kept us amused by letting us play on her typewriter. We only had a few hours with her. We waited in silence every day for the slamming of the front door at six o'clock. Nan would grab me very hard and kiss me on the cheek, because she knew what we were about to face next.

Shaun would grasp her skirt. 'I don't want to go downstairs! Can't we stay with you, Nanny?' he would wail.

Even then, I would try to mother him. I pulled him away from Nan's skirt and towards me, focusing on Nan all the time and trying not to cry myself. By now, I was just seven, but even at that young age I felt I had to make up to him for the mother that he had lost. I was convinced that it was my fault, although I still could not remember what I had done. I was the oldest, so I took the blame.

Getting ready for school became an ordeal now, because my father got me ready. Every morning I would tiptoe down the stairs. The moment his eyes viewed me, they were filled with hatred.

'Come here!' he'd growl.

My stomach churned as I neared my way over to him.

'Don't wet yourself, please, don't wet yourself!' I kept thinking to myself.

I would feel myself shrink back as he reached out and grabbed my arm. His grip was so strong that my arms always bruised immediately. I could feel tears stinging the back of my eyes, but I would not allow them to come to the surface. I had already learned that he could not tolerate tears.

'Right, turn around, you . . . ' Again he swore at me.

With my back to him I waited for the brush to slam into my head. The prongs would dig deep, hard into my skull, and then be dragged down over my shoulders and back. The pain was sharp and intense. I could feel every strand of hair being stretched to its full capacity. Over and over again the brush slammed in, until the movements became less laboured and my head was throbbing with the pain. When every tangle was out, he would get a rubber band, pulling my hair into a tight knot and gathering it all through the centre. My face felt stretched like a fitted sheet over a mattress. I could not move for the pain. Eventually, he let go of me and made me sit and eat my breakfast. Sometimes he would be quiet and other times he would make horrible comments – interspersed with swear words.

'If you two were not . . . here, I would have some sort of a life! Instead I'm stuck here with you two . . . ! If you two had died at birth, I would not be stuck with you like a rope around my neck!'

Day in and day out, it became routine: the comments, the hatred. The consolation of my day was when I saw Nan. As much as my father hated me, she loved me. She made my days bearable.

As time went by, I knew what to expect, what time of day to expect it, and I knew how to act in order to get through the incident. I learned from my mistakes. If I cried, I was punished; if I wet myself, I was punished. I knew what rooms in the house to venture into and at what times. I was never allowed into the sitting-room at any time of the day, and I was never to go into my father's bedroom. But then, I was to suffer another blow. My father banned me from going upstairs after school to see Nan. I came home from school and even though I knew that she was upstairs, I dare not disobey his rule. Nan knew, too, that if he caught me, it would cost me dearly. As much as it hurt her, she had to accept things as they were – for my sake, and my brother's. Not only did the house become a virtual prison for me, but also for my nan, to whom it actually belonged. Nan remained upstairs and I remained downstairs, never allowed to pass on the stairs.

Sundays was bath-time. My father would fill the bath with scalding hot water, leaving me with a stinging sensation all over my body. He had a long-handled scrubbing brush. He made us stand up whilst he scrubbed us from head to foot, as if he were trying to rip the flesh off our bones. The bristles felt sharp against our skin, leaving long red marks, adding to our misery. Then he would wash our hair; my neck would ache for hours afterwards because of the harshness with which he drove the shampoo into my head. It was like he had found a way of releasing his frustration. He kneaded and pressed my skull and Shaun's with ardent determination. After the ordeal of the bath was over, and he had dried us down with towels – with the same fierceness – he would cut our nails. This experience was particularly frightening for us.

My father would make us hold out our hands in front of us. Shaun had always been nervous and he bit his nails right down to the quick from an early age. Even so, my father made sure that there was something to cut . . . even if it is was Shaun's fingertips. If either of us flinched, he would take a wooden clothes brush and it would be rapped across our knuckles. Once he grabbed my arm so hard, as I tried to pull away from him, that the socket hurt for days. When he began to cut, the pain was intense and made me feel sick but his grip was so strong that I could do nothing but watch. Tears welled up as the scissors cut through the skin, and blood became visible. I forced myself not to cry. When it was Shaun's turn, he would scream in pain, but my father would clench his teeth and cut with more intensity.

Then, I would watch in horror as the wooden clothes brush was wielded. It was a good three inches thick, and it came down, right across Shaun's knuckles, ten times. I flinched as I heard the wood hit the bone. Shaun was always made to go up to his bedroom afterwards and write 'I must not bite my nails' one hundred times. His hands, by this time, were totally purple and blue, his knuckles swollen to twice their normal size, with dried blood embedded in his fingertips.

Later, I would creep into his bedroom so that my father could not hear me. I'd cradle my brother's head in my hands and he would cry for a long time. I nursed his fingers with cotton wool and warm water and then I would write his lines for him, trying to make my writing look like his. He was only five and his writing was still shaky and sometimes illegible. I knew if I had been caught doing it, my father would punish me, but there was no way that Shaun could write those lines – with his swollen hands, he could not even hold a pen. No, it was up to me to take the risk and, every week, I did.

One day, we came home from school as usual. As we went into the house, we heard noises, like grunting and heavy breathing. Then we heard laughter. I thought Nan had the television on too loud. But the noise seemed to be coming from my father's bedroom.

I pushed the door open and there he was, in bed with a woman. My father snatched up the sheet, covered himself, jumped out of the bed, and made his way towards me. I grabbed Shaun. We both ran into the breakfast room and waited. The moment before my father entered the room seemed endless. All of a sudden the door flew open and there he stood.

'Don't you *dare* come in to that room again, do you hear me? Don't you dare!'

I thought that he was going to slap me, but instead he just turned around, his bare back revealing the muscles and the broadness of his shoulders.

After a while, the woman appeared. I didn't recognise her.

'This is your Aunty Margo,' said my father, brusquely. 'She's going to be staying with us from now on.'

I was puzzled. I did not know I had an Aunty! She peered at us through her glasses but never said a word.

I had a feeling that life with this woman was not going to be easy.

Everything seemed to be happening too fast. My mother had gone and I was no longer allowed to see Nan. Now we had a new person to deal with; someone who was nothing like my mother. This woman was a stranger.

One night, courage or sheer desperation, I do not know which, made me come out of my bedroom. I crept along the landing. I could hear the faint sounds of voices coming from my nan's television. I moved very slowly towards her kitchen. The corridor seemed never-ending. My heart was banging so loudly in my chest that I thought the whole neighbourhood must have heard it. I carefully stepped over the creaking floor boards. Carefully, I opened the door. There she was, sitting at her typewriter.

'Nanny!' I whispered.

She was surprised, but pleased to see me – I could tell.

'Darling! Does your father know you're here?'

I shook my head and clung to her. It felt so good, that familiar smell of lavender on her clothes . . . I had so much I wanted to say to her, but I couldn't speak. I just wanted to enjoy the moment. That was to be the first night of many. I would sneak out of my bedroom late at night to see her, and she began to leave her door ajar so that I did not have to worry about it making a noise as I opened it. My night-time escapades kept me going. The sheer anticipation of seeing her kept me alive, breathing. I got through each day, knowing that I could see her at night.

Then one afternoon, when I came home from school, I opened the front door and heard voices. Was it my father and Aunty Margo again? I tip-toed the length of the downstairs corridor and edged towards my father's bedroom. The voices did not get any louder. I took a deep breath and opened the door. No one was there. Where are the voices coming from? I wandered into the breakfast room; again, no one there.

'What's happening, sis?' asked Shaun.

My attention was drawn upstairs to my nan's kitchen. Nervously, I started to climb the stairs, fearing that at any moment, my father would come through the front door and catch me. Another fear rose up in me. What if it was my father's voice, speaking to my nan? I would certainly die if I went in and found him there!

'Nanny, it's us! Are you there?' I waited for her reply, but none came.

With a sudden spurt of energy, I ran up the rest of the stairs. The voices were coming from her television. I edged the door open and there she was, sitting on her chair, eyes wide open.

'Nanny!'

She had been sick all down her blue dress. I shook her and wondered why she did not answer me. I tried to clean the mess off her dress before my father saw her. I could not bear the thought that he should see her like that. I was frightened. I could not get her to speak to me. She just sat there, eyes wide, staring at the ceiling. All I could do was sit with her and hold her hand. Tears began to roll down my face. I did not care any more if my father saw them. I did not think of Shaun, on his own downstairs, or that time was passing by. My thoughts were too wrapped up in my nan. Nothing I did or said brought her back to me. I didn't hear my father's footsteps and I didn't hear him coming up behind me.

'Come here, Shireen!' I glanced at his outstretched hand.

'No, I don't think Nanny's very well. I'm staying with her till she wakes up,' I said.

He came over to me, bent down towards Nanny and rested his hand over her eyes. When he took his hand away her eyes were shut. He gripped my arm and pulled me away from her.

'No! Leave me alone! Nanny needs me! Go away!' I cried.

I felt no fear as I fought with him. All I wanted was to be near to my nan. I began to sob uncontrollably. He let go of me and left the room, and I was left alone with her. For a while longer, I sat there beside her; I did not understand what was happening. Why did she not respond when I called her? I wanted her, I needed her. Panic was all I felt that afternoon. I watched as a man came into Nan's kitchen, someone I had never seen before; he was followed by my father. My strength had run out now and I could not fight with my father again, so quietly and submissively, I left the kitchen.

I knew, that day, although no one ever told me, that Nan was gone forever. I loved her so much but I was angry with her; how could she, of all people, leave me now? I looked at her lifeless body and all I wanted to do was shake her until she smiled that same smile that warmed my heart. I wanted those eyes, those blank eyes that had been staring up to the ceiling, to focus on me again. But deep down, I knew from that moment that I would never see that smile again, or sit on my nan's lap, tinkling away at the keys of her typewriter. Whatever life was going to throw at me and my brother, we would have to deal with it on our own.

Chapter 3

Margo

By the time I was ten, my life was as grey and dingy as a rainy day. There was no laughter, there was no fun. All I knew was pain and disappointment. The circumstances of my life had forced me to grow up very quickly. After all, there was Shaun to consider. I had to be his mother.

I missed Nan desperately, but Shaun missed her as much as I did and had grown to be very clingy towards me. I couldn't talk to him about Nan, otherwise he would start to snivel. I had to be on my guard if he did, because if our father had heard that, he would have slapped us both. His slaps came from nowhere and jarred my skull so much that it felt like my head and shoulders might part company. The stinging sensation would make my eyes start to pour with water. I quickly had to wipe the tears away before my father noticed – otherwise I would get another slap and a warning.

'Shut the . . . up before I hit you again, you little . . .' He used words that I never heard in other company; they disturbed me as they echoed around my brain.

There were times when I would wake up in the middle of the night. I could see my nan staring up at the

17

skies. I could see myself shaking her. The screaming in my head was so loud that I would wake up, warm and clammy – and realise what I had done. Quickly, I would take my sheets and blanket to my nan's unused kitchen, quietly wash the sheets and return to my bedroom. One day my father heard me and came up the stairs. When he saw what I was doing, down came his hand, right across my face.

'You dirty . . .!' he snarled.

Without realising, I wet myself again. This time there came a blow to my stomach. He pulled my hair and dragged me down to the ground, using my hair to wipe up the liquid. Then came the kick, swift and sharp. After that, when I lay on my side, it hurt. I buried my face deep in my pillow and cried silent tears, making it as wet as the sheets that I was now forced to sleep on. The next day I was aching with all that happened the night before, but I still went to school and tried to act normally. I tried to make myself invisible, just like I did at home. I did not want anyone asking me awkward questions. If anyone had said anything to my father, my life would not have been worth living. Not that it was worth living anyway.

Whilst other children were out playing in the park and enjoying themselves, I was cleaning. I was now my father's housekeeper. I hoovered, polished, washed and pegged clothes out on the line. That was my Saturday morning routine.

Aunty Margo had taken up residence in my father's bedroom. One day, the door was ajar. I peeped in and glimpsed the dressing table. All kinds of brown bottles were lined up on it, in a regimental style. I wondered what they were for. My mother had never had bottles like that on her dressing table.

'Some kind of perfume, maybe,' I said to myself.

Aunty Margo did not like Shaun or me, and she seemed to take great delight in getting us into trouble. Every Saturday morning, she would inspect the house after I had vacuumed and polished; then she would look at the shirts that I had washed, always searching for something to complain about. Another task she set us was to go to the Post Office and collect the Family Allowance. If we were a minute late by her calculations, she would threaten us with the ultimate: 'Wait till your father gets home!'

Consequently, Saturdays were hellish. I would hear the sounds of children running past in the morning on their way to the park, or the swimming pool, or the cinema, and wonder what it would be like just to be free to do what you liked. Television became my greatest friend. My life revolved around it. It was all I had.

When my father came home, we hid in our bedrooms, pretending we were doing homework. If he did not hear us, he left us alone. If he heard us, there was trouble. If we used the bathroom and had to pull the chain, we used to hold our breath just in case he heard it. Our lives were an interruption for him. Some days, we did not need to do anything at all to make him angry; he would call us down from our bedrooms, and when he did that, we knew he was in a bad mood. We became his punch bags. He used to grab Shaun's hair and drive his head into the wall. Then he would turn his attention to me. He would hit us, relentlessly, using his fists. When these sessions were over, we would both go up to our bedrooms, each silent and numb with pain. My stomach would hurt where he had punched me and my back would be bruised. But never did I allow myself to cry, even at such a young age; I would not give him the satisfaction. Not only that, but I feared that seeing my tears, he might repeat things.

At school I began to lie about what I had done at the weekends. I would make up stories about how I had gone to London or to the seaside. I would pretend I had done some of the things I had seen on TV. Soon I developed a world of fantasy that was so real to me that I was able to escape at any given moment. I would slip away and become one of the characters I'd seen in a film. I found that I could drift in and out of this world whenever I wanted to. I had found the power of escapism – in this new world, I always came first. I was loved and cherished, never hurt or abused; just loved.

One Sunday morning, my father got us up early and told us to get dressed.

'I want you to put your best clothes on. We're going to meet Aunty Margo's stepmother, so be on your best behaviour. And remember, both of you, call her *Aunty* Margo. Don't you dare call her "Margo" in public,' he said as he left the room, slamming the door behind him.

After breakfast, we marched down to our local railway station. We had to go through the park to get to it. I loved the sounds and smells of the park, with all the trees lining the pathways. I watched as the children were being pushed on the swings by their mums and dads. I could hear their shrieks of laughter as they came hurtling down the slides and their cheers when they were thrown up high on the wooden rocking horse. I began to dawdle as I watched them, only to be brought back to reality by a hand across the back of my head.

It was bitterly cold on the station platform. I stared at the mouth of the dark tunnel which looked totally menacing to me, and I shivered. We waited for what seemed like an age. Then I heard the sound of roaring, and drumming. Shaun and I looked at each other as we felt the vibration under our feet. A long blue and green train emerged from the tunnel and I gasped. I had seen trains from a distance, from my nan's kitchen, but had never got this close to one. I had even fantasised about them – what it would be like to be on one, taking me away to another place. I was so transfixed by the train that I did not see my father come towards me. He pulled at my arm.

'You stupid idiot! Don't go near those yellow lines or you'll be swept under the train! Do you hear me?'

There was a loud whistle and the train doors began to jolt open. My father and Aunty Margo climbed into one of the compartments and we dutifully followed. Excitement began to rise up inside me. After all, I had never got on a train before.

Shaun and I sat facing my father and Aunty Margo. I looked round. Every seat was filled. Some of the people smiled at me, but no one spoke. Eventually, I broke the silence as I stood to take off my coat.

'Margo, does your mum live down by the sea?'

I had not thought about what I had said and in a split second, my father's fist hit my cheek, sending me reeling to the floor. It felt as though my eye was about to split. The pain was excruciating; my jaw hurt badly. I got to my feet and all the people were staring at me. I kept my head bowed, too ashamed to look at them, but I could feel their eyes upon me. The train was now moving and I found it difficult to balance. I had to walk past my father again to get to my seat; the train jolted suddenly, and I fell into his lap. He gripped my arm. I flinched but did not dare look into his eyes. He threw me into my seat.

'Didn't I tell you not to call her "Margo"? *Aunty* Margo! Sit down and just shut up. I don't want to hear you for the rest of the journey. Do you hear me?'

I kept opening and closing my mouth, the pain in my jaw was so intense. I was frightened because it felt like it was broken. It kept jarring and going stiff. All my effort went into not crying. I just kept my eyes fixed on the scenery that was flashing past quickly. I could hear a high-pitched whistling in my ears but it was soon replaced by the constant drumming sound of the wheels on the track.

At our journey's end, we arrived at *Aunty* Margo's stepmother's place. It was a large Victorian house, with many windows. As we came to the front door my father warned us again about what we were to call Margo. But I had learned my lesson. I had no intention of calling her simply 'Margo' again – leaving off the 'Aunty' tag that was so important to him . . . in public.

We were welcomed in. I was so surprised to see everything in one room. In one corner was a sink with a mirror over it. At the back of the room was a tiny kitchen. The fridge, cooker and cupboards were all miniature in size. In the other corner near the window was the stepmother's bed, covered in a pink bedspread, and there were flowers in a vase on the windowsill. Although I liked the room, I was not sure about the stern old woman. However, I noticed that my father was very quiet and reserved in her presence – it was unusual to see him like this.

After what seemed like hours of talking, the old woman got up and suggested that we go to a nearby café for lunch. We arrived at the sea front and I heard the wonderful sound of waves crashing against rocks. Shaun and I leaned over the barrier that divided the rocks from the pavement, and watched the water coming higher and higher. It was a feeling of sheer freedom, with the wind in my hair and the salty breeze in my face; the freshness of the air here was so different to where I had come from. I was so caught up with my surroundings that I had not realised that my father and the two women were now some distance away. When at last I did notice, I was amazed that he had not shouted at us not to run off.

After a while, my father called out.

'Come on kids, we're going to eat! Are you hungry?'

Shaun and I looked at each other, puzzled at how nice he was being.

We reached the café and sat at a table near a window. I kept gazing out at the sea. I could feel my face glowing with the cold.

The day soon came to an end. We said 'goodbye' to Margo's stepmother and made our way back to the station. All things considered, it had been a good day. Even our father had been good to us. I could not understand the change in his attitude. However, it was an attitude towards Shaun and I that only came out when we were in the presence of other people.

I sat on the train that evening wishing that the wheels would not race so fast, as I was in no hurry to go back to Croydon and the dreary familiarity. Croydon seemed so stark and uninviting compared to the coast. The cleanness of the air and the freshness of the water had made me feel alive and hopeful, whereas my house was full of hate and anger – I couldn't call it a 'home'.

I never knew why, but Margo was particularly vicious towards my brother. Sometimes she would come home early from work and would spend the rest of the day in bed. She would call out to us as we came through the front door, demanding that we make her a cup of coffee. When we took it in to her, she would snap at us to leave it on the dressing table, alongside the little brown bottles that were always neatly lined up. My eyes would linger on the long names, I tried to pronounce them but there were too many letters.

One evening, I could smell burning. It was coming from my father's bedroom. As I got nearer, I could hear

Margo crying; it was like a child's cry. I pushed the door open to see her pulling at her nightdress, as if she were trying to get it off her body. She had a gold lighter in her hand, and was flicking it again and again. Tears of frustration were running down her cheeks. Each time she flicked it, a flame would appear and she would hold it to her nightdress. I could see lots of burn holes. Instinctively, I knew I had to get the lighter out of her hands. We fought but she was a lot stronger than me and she knocked me to the floor. Then Shaun came in and we both fought with her. She was screaming and shouting at us.

'Wait till your father comes home!'

Her threats meant nothing at that point; all I could think of was the lighter. I forgot that my actions would have consequences. Eventually, she dropped the lighter on the floor. I took my chance and scurried over, picking it up with one swift movement. Then Shaun and I fled the bedroom.

As we ran out, the phone rang. I picked it up and heard my mother's voice.

'Mum, Mum, she's setting fire to herself!' I screamed down the phone.

Then the front door opened and my father came in. Hearing Margo screaming and raving, he came charging over to me, and ripped the receiver away. His hand came down, hitting my face with such force that I flew across the floor and hit the wall.

'Don't you ever pick up that phone if it rings! Leave it, do you hear?'

He went into his bedroom and shut the door. Shaun and I raced up the stairs and hid in our rooms. We could hear shouting and swearing. Neither of us dared say anything; we just cowered behind the door, waiting for his footsteps to come up the stairs, but they never did.

Once all the confusion and the shouting had died down, Shaun and I sat in my bedroom, discussing all that had happened. I began to think about my mother's voice on the other end of the phone. I wondered if she knew all that was happening. I had made a conscious effort not to think about her because it was too painful, but now that I had heard her voice, all I wanted was my mum. Tears welled up but I squeezed my eyes shut and ordered them to disappear.

That was not to be the last time that Margo behaved in a very strange manner. I came home another day and found her on the downstairs kitchen floor. All around her were saucepans. The clank of metal was loud as she put them in a neat pile. I watched as she then took them all down again, and arranged them on the floor in some sort of pattern. That pattern must have meant something to her, because she took her time, stacking them up, taking them down. This routine went on for ages, over and over again. Eventually, as if tired by the whole thing, she lifted them all up and slung them in the bottom cupboard. She then began to crawl on the floor, like a baby. Shaun and I stared at each other, bewildered by what we were witnessing. We tried to call her but she seemed to be totally oblivious to our presence in the room.

This just seemed like one more incident in my life that I could not understand. The arguments between Margo and my father grew more and more intense and her behavior became more bizarre. She walked around the house in her dressing-gown in the middle of the day, talking to herself, and then shouting into the air. She didn't seem to know my brother and I were watching her.

Margo was, of course, very ill indeed. But we didn't know it.

Chapter 4

All Too Much

One morning, my father burst into the room.

'You're going to see your . . . mother today, get dressed!' He spun round and slammed the door behind him.

I stood for a few moments taking in what he had just said. Then he came back into the room.

'I don't want you telling her anything about what goes on in this house! You don't mention your Aunty Margo, nothing! If I find out that you've said something you shouldn't, it will be the worse for you, do you hear?' He seemed even more angry than usual.

I could not believe it. I was going to see my mother again! I couldn't wait. I was glued to Shaun's bedroom window, which faced the main road. At last – at long, long last – she came. Margo stayed in her bedroom and my father glared at us as we walked past him. I flinched, waiting for the inevitable, but it didn't come. The front door got nearer and nearer, then with one last sprint Shaun and I fled our place of captivity.

'Well, you two,' said my mother, 'how have you been?'

I felt strange; I was happy to see her, but I felt angry at the same time. She felt soft and squishy, warm with a smell of soap. I cuddled up closer to her, melting as she put her arm around me and kissed me.

At our mother's new home, we had to climb a flight of stairs to the top part of the house. Tentatively, Shaun and I went into the living room. It was snug, with fluffy rugs everywhere. It was very warm, unlike our house, which felt cold even in the middle of summer. My little sister quickly led us into her bedroom.

I stared around. I couldn't believe my eyes. She had loads of toys everywhere. White painted units held an array of pretty clothes; there were little china ornaments on top of the cupboards. Everywhere was pink and fluffy, a little girl's dream. Debbie was five now, and had short blonde hair and blue eyes. She was excited to see us, running round her bedroom showing off all her toys and books. I kept looking around her room in disbelief. I could feel the tears coming, but I quickly blinked them away. I wished I had not come.

My mother had a home now, so why did she not come back for me? I wished somebody would just tell me what I did wrong! I sat in Debbie's bedroom, wondering why we were with him and Debbie was with her. A feeling of total abandonment washed over me.

All that afternoon, I desperately wanted to speak to my mother, and ask her all the questions that were queuing up in my mind. Instead, I sat in silence. She did not try to explain away the last five years; instead, she tried her best to make the experience of our meeting again totally enjoyable. Hurriedly, she laid the table with shiny knives, forks and spoons. There was every kind of jam, honey and marmalade you could think of, different types of cakes and biscuits, crisps of all shapes and varieties . . . nothing like Shaun and I were used to.

I watched as my brother and sister tucked into the feast; they were happy and giggling, but my appetite was gone, sent away by the awful churning going on in my mind and stomach.

'It's time to get your coats on darlings, better get you home!'

My heart sank at her words. By now, I felt very strange indeed. Part of me wanted to stay longer with my mother but another part of me did not. I wanted to see her but it was so painful to leave. I wanted so desperately to speak to her, but knowing that I dare not say a word, I got into the car, silent, angry and terribly hurt. I ached to speak to her before I left. The mixture of anger and pain intensified inside of me. I just did not understand.

Why couldn't I stay with her? She'd made a home now; why wasn't there any room in it for me and Shaun? Why was she making us go back to that house – with him?

I kept forcing myself to be strong and not let any tears fall. I did not want my father to see me crying as I waved goodbye to my mother, watching her car disappear from view.

Once inside the house, Shaun and I walked past my father and went upstairs. From behind my bedroom door, we strained our ears to hear what was going on. My father was talking to Margo.

He came upstairs, then, and questioned us about what we had said to our mother. It was as if he was interrogating us. I was able to say, truthfully, that I had said nothing. I also asked him when we would see her again, but got no reply.

A few weeks later, I received a letter from her. I sat on the end of my bed and read it intently. As I scanned the pages, I could see no explanation as to why we could only see her on one short visit. I threw the piece of paper across the room, in anger; then, I cried into my pillow. It may have been an inanimate object but right then it offered more comfort than anyone with a heartbeat. I cried into it for hours, pressing it harder and harder over my mouth, muffling the sound of my screams. I hated being with my father. I had convinced myself that my mother did not want me any more because she had her blue-eyed, blonde-haired daughter now. I hated Debbie, too. She had everything – I had nothing.

From that time, I made up my mind that I was going to run away from home. If my mother wasn't going to take me with her, then I would run away and be with her. Surely, she would not make me go back to my father, if she knew what was happening? I could not understand why she wouldn't talk to me about anything that mattered. I did not see the fear that she, too, was living under, because of this man. I loved her so much, and I wanted to be a part of her life, but I was eaten up inside with this pain. I woke up with it and I went to bed with it. It never left me. It was worse than a toothache. I kept thinking of my sister and her pretty pink things.

Night after night I used to lie awake until the early hours, planning to run away. Thoughts of living a new life with my mother and sister made me so excited I could hardly bear it. There would be freedom to do all the things I wanted to do: go bike-riding, swimming, everything that I could only dream of.

In the meantime, Margo's health went from bad to worse. One time, I found her on the edge of her bed, surrounded by her little brown bottles. All the contents had been spilled out, different coloured tablets of all shapes and sizes. She was counting them methodically, placing them into their appropriate bottles. Then she would tip them out again. Unaware of my presence in the room, she just kept counting. I did not know that she was mentally ill. Because nothing in my life was normal I didn't realise that what she was doing was abnormal. One moment she would be calm, the next she would be hysterical, pulling her hair out of her own head in big clumps.

My free time was so wrapped up in housework that even if I wanted to, there was little time to make friends. So I had given up the thought. Then one Saturday, whilst I was going to get the Family Allowance, I passed a house where lots of children were playing in the front garden. They were laughing and running around, doing the kind of things that *normal* children do. They looked happy. As I got near to them, they stopped to speak to me. One girl, who was about my age, came up to me and introduced herself.

'I'm Beverley. You're in my class, aren't you?' she said.

'Yes. My name's Shireen.'

We began to talk.

The front door to their house was open and a lovely smell of clean washing began to float out from the kitchen. We talked for ages about school, music, and other things. It was so nice to have someone to talk to, someone who seemed to like me. I suddenly realised what the time was and made my apologies, then ran. I had to make up for the lost time. As I was waiting for the Family Allowance, I kept thinking about Beverley, and began to get excited. I had really enjoyed talking to someone my own age.

For the first time in my miserable existence, I had a friend. We spent lots of time together at school. I was no longer filled with thoughts about running away to my mother; instead I was always thinking about how I could sneak out of the house unnoticed.

One Saturday morning, I woke up to find the sun blazing through the window. Beverley and I had spoken about what we were going to do. I ran to the bathroom and washed and dressed in record time. Then I got the vacuum cleaner out of the cupboard and hoovered. I threw my father's shirts and our school uniforms into the twin tub and stood impatiently whilst they swirled around in the soapy water.

I had not realised that Shaun had left a pen inside his pocket. When the machine stopped, I opened the lid and gasped. There were blue tints all over Shaun's school uniform – and my father's white shirts. Panic seized me.

'He'll go mad!' I fumbled in the cupboard under the sink, frantically searching for something to get the stains out of the material. 'Aha – bleach!'

I grabbed the bottle and tipped a load into the machine and switched on. I left it and went away to continue vacuuming, hoping that the stains would come out. And that's when I began to pray.

'If there's a God up there, I hope you'll take pity on me and do something!'

The stains were still there. I pegged the washing out on the line and hoped in some feeble way that the sun would get the stains out.

I went to Beverley's but I didn't enjoy it. My stomach churned all day. I knew when my father found his shirts, he'd probably kill me.

'Right little ray of sunshine, aren't we!' Beverley said, apparently put out that her playmate wasn't as much fun as usual.

'I'm sorry.' I tried to smile. 'I've – er – got a lot on my mind today.'

Her mother heard that. 'What on earth can a little mite like you have on your mind that is so terrible?' she asked.

I really wanted to tell her, but I couldn't. I loved being with them, but I could never afford to tell them about my life. Even though Beverley kept asking me about my mother, I just told her that I did not have one, which in a way was true; anyway, it kept her quiet. I found that easier than having to explain that my mother had in fact left me behind.

When I went home, I hoped some miracle had happened and that the stains had been bleached out by the sun's rays, but no; the shirts were still the same. 'Please,' I whispered, 'please, someone tell me what to do!' And then I heard Margo, indoors, complaining loudly.

'That little . . . was hoovering at eight o'clock this morning! It's supposed to be my day off!'

I went in. She still had her night clothes on. She had been in them all day. My father was with her. And then he approached me.

I backed away, placing my body between him and the shirts. I started to cry as I saw the anger in his eyes.

'Come here, you little . . . !' One of his hands gripped my arm and then I watched his other hand come down. Only this time it had changed from a hand to a fist. He caught me under the chin. I felt my eyes bulge in my head and my jaw burned. I reeled across the floor, fell, and my head hit the radiator. For a moment I could not see properly. My eyes were blurry, nothing was visible. I could see a dark image coming towards me. I knew it was him but I did not have the strength to move. Then his foot, clad with Doc Marten boots – boots he had to wear in the warehouse, where he worked – came up to my ribs.

'You little . . . ! Why should I have to come home to this every night? I work my fingers to the bone to keep you, you little . . . !'

I felt the breath leave my body. Was this it, would I die tonight? I hoped so. In my thoughts I begged to be set free. I *wanted* him to kill me.

But he didn't. At last, I struggled to my bedroom. Although many hours had passed, I could still not see properly. I had to feel my way to my room and stumbled about as I tried to get to my bed. My head was spinning and my ribs felt like they were broken. Fear that I was going blind made me cry myself to sleep.

The next morning my ribs felt like they had caved in; I'd been sick throughout the night.

After that, my eyesight and my hearing grew steadily worse. My schoolwork was suffering. My school had written to my father voicing concerns over my inability to see the blackboard and hear the teachers, even though they'd placed me at the front. They suggested that he took me for an eye test – the result of which revealed that I had a stigmatism in my right eye. I had to have glasses from then on.

I began to have regular hearing tests as my hearing was worsening, too. The results of the hearing test showed that I had a form of tinnitus, a buzzing in my ears that was constant – and with no cure. They questioned my father as to whether I had taken a blow to the head at any time. My father flatly denied it. I also had to have a full medical check-up at the local surgery. With my father outside the door, I nervously answered all of the doctor's questions, never daring to disclose any secrets. They were unable to diagnose why I was suffering with severe headaches – I was eleven years old and on six painkillers a day. I wore glasses and my hearing was rapidly deteriorating. With all the signs in front of them, no one ever questioned the deterioration of my health. They just assumed I was a sickly child. After all, I had cold after cold and lots of mouth ulcers.

I had cross country after school one day and came home later than expected. With her usual zeal to inform on me as soon as my father came home from work, Margo started: 'I've got enough on my plate! I don't need to be worrying about your . . . kids! *She* never came home until five this evening. I thought you were going to have a word with her about her disobedience!' She blazed on and on.

Suddenly, my father charged at me. I was so stunned, I did not have time to think, it happened so fast. The hand came down and I flew, once again, across the floor to the other side of the room. I lay there for a second, unable to move. I eventually got up and wearily made my way to my bedroom. Even after all the tests and checks I had gone through at the hospital and with the doctors, even with me being on tablets, he still did not relent! I lay on my bed, just wishing I was free.

The next moment, I picked up the bottle of painkillers and went to the bathroom. I tipped all of the tablets into the palm of my hand and stared at them. It was all too much; everything was just too hard: worrying about my father, my health, my brother, whether I would get the washing dry in time; worrying about what Margo would do to get me into trouble. I had not been without a headache for weeks. I turned the tap on and filled a glass. And I swallowed every single tablet.

I had done it. At least thirty tablets were making their way down to the place where those little butterflies had taken up residence on my first day of school, and had never left. Soon, they, like me, would be put to sleep for ever.

I went to my bedroom and put my coat on. I could not stay any more. All I wanted to do was die quietly. But I had to be quick; I didn't know how long the tablets would take to work, and I didn't want to be found in the house. If I was found by someone else, they might come and take Shaun away to a better life. Shaun! It hit me – I was about to leave him all alone! I hurriedly went to his bedroom and told him to put his coat on because we were getting out. I could feel my legs starting to shake.

'Shaun, I've had enough of this place. I'm leaving.' My heart seemed to be jumping. 'If you want to come with me, you'd better hurry. I don't have much time.'

As we got to the top of the landing we could hear my father and Margo, talking. As quietly as we could, Shaun and I left the house, stepping softly into the chilly evening air. And then we began to run, turning round every so often to see if my father was behind us. I fell to the ground at one point, scraping my knees. Clumsily, I got up again. My head was becoming fuzzy, and my eyesight was blurred. It was dark now, and the street lights were on, but to me, the trees lining the road were just a mass of black; then, as I tried to focus, the lights mingled with the branches, and I felt like I was inside a kaleidoscope. Unable to think clearly by now, I told Shaun that I needed to rest.

We reached the park where Beverley and I had played together with her brothers. I remembered a huge hut that seated about fifty people, and decided that this would be the perfect place to shelter. We ran to the park entrance, but the gate was locked.

'There's only one way to get in there, sis. We've got to climb over!' said Shaun.

I looked at the railings but couldn't make them out properly. I fumbled around, trying to find the top of the metal posts, so that I could swing my legs over. How I managed it I will never know, but somehow I jumped the fence. I hit the ground with real force, and fell face down on the wet grass. It felt like I was doing things in slow motion.

Shaun put his arm around my waist and we both headed for the hut. I lay on the bench. My head was spinning, and I could feel immense pressure behind my eyes. The smell of urine in that hut made me gag; I began to be sick. Drained, cold and not caring any more,

I waited for death. I started to tremble violently and my teeth were rattling. Shaun just sat on the bench rocking backwards and forwards, trying to keep warm. Again and again I vomited – all the drugs that I had taken were being expelled from my system. And then I fell asleep.

I woke up with a start. Voices! Shaun and I hid in the corner of the hut. I could see lights flashing; the voices were getting nearer. I pulled my brother close to me.

'Shush, be very quiet, it might be him!'

Two men . . . was one of them our father? We kept ducking every time the light came our way. The men were obviously looking for something – or someone – and soon moved on in their search. When they did, we slipped out of the hut and raced to the edge of the park.

'Come on, he might come back! We'd better go somewhere else!' We both grasped the railings and leapt over.

There was a car parked under a nearby street light. We could see the figures of two men inside. We walked straight past, without realising that they were the men who had been in the park – or even registering that it was in fact a police car.

One of them opened the car door. 'Hey, you kids!'

Shaun and I looked at each other and without saying one word, we ran. The car cruised alongside us.

'Come on, you two, stop running!' said one of the policemen, as he wound down the window. 'Do you know what time of night it is? You shouldn't be out here on your own.'

Inside the police car, the men were very kind to us.

'Well, what are you two doing out here at this time of night, eh?' said one of them.

'We've run away from home!' Shaun blurted out. 'My sister's taken loads of tablets and doesn't feel well. She keeps being sick!'

'Is that true, young lady? Have you taken loads of tablets?' asked the other policeman. 'We'd better get you home. Your parents will be very worried about you!'

I didn't say anything. I don't think they believed my brother, and I was not about to volunteer any information. By that stage in my young life, I already had a real mistrust of just about everybody.

'Where do you live, then? We'll give you a ride home!'

I couldn't believe it. These men were about to take me back to the very place that I had run away from and they were not even going to ask me why I'd run away in the first place! They just wanted to get us back home where we belonged and then they could carry on with their night.

We waited for the car to stop outside our front door. There were no bars on the windows or bolts on the doors, but there might as well have been. Slowly and fearfully, Shaun and I got out of the car. My mouth went dry and my palms started to sweat and it wasn't because of the tablets. They were now all gone, along with the effects, and I was very lucid. By now I had resigned myself to the fact that it didn't matter that the tablets hadn't worked; it would only be a matter of time before my father killed me anyway.

One of the policemen knocked on the door. There my father stood, the muscles in his arms were bulging through his white T-shirt.

'Good evening, sir!' said the policeman, pleasantly. 'I believe these are your children!'

My father looked at us. At first, he seemed bewildered. Then he smiled – broadly.

'Yes, officer! Where were they?'

The police officer had his hand on my back and was pushing me gently towards the door.

'They were coming out of the park. It's a bit late for them to be out, sir!'

'Sorry, officer, it won't happen again . . . you can take my word for it!' my father said.

Panic-stricken, Shaun and I scrambled up to our bedrooms. We knew what was in store. I just prayed that the policemen would talk to him for ever. It kept him away from us.

But then I heard his footsteps. The steps came closer and closer to my bedroom. Tears began to stream down my face, and my head began to throb once again. The door burst open and there he stood.

'So you wanted to run away, did you? Thought you'd go to *her*, did you? Well, if you think that she can take care of you better than I can, go!' He turned around and left the room.

'Was that it?' I could not believe what had happened; but on this occasion, he didn't hit me and he didn't hit Shaun. We never did know why.

Chapter 5

Holy Books

We got to see our mum about three or four times a year. The more I saw her, the more difficult it became for me. I loved to see her but I did not want to just visit her. I wanted to stay with her, to belong, to wake up to the smell of freshly washed linen and have fluffy toys everywhere. Instead, all I had of my mother were the letters that she would write after she saw us. I was already angry at the world and that anger was escalating. I was even angry with myself. I knew I should love my mother, but I was so angry with her and I couldn't understand why. I *did* love her; I always had, but lately, since I had been seeing her now and again, I was beginning to have feelings of hate for her. I hated not being able to talk to her about my life. I hated looking through the window of her life, seeing all the nice things that she had, whilst my own life was crumbling.

It was all I could do to get through the days when I saw her. I would leave my house of hell, with all its darkness and rage, and enter a different sort of hell, in her house – the house that was filled with sweet sensations that gouged away at my heart. The pain that she inflicted seemed worse than the physical pain that my father caused. I felt that to her, I was nothing more than the child that she had thrown away. She had my sister and there was no need for her to come back for me. My brother and I had become visitors in her life; we were no longer family. There were no pictures of us on the walls and no paintings that we had done stuck to her fridge.

As if washing and ironing and taking care of my brother were not enough responsibility for me to cope with, my father had added more. Whilst it was the responsibility of children my age to make sure that the rabbit hutch or the guinea pig cage was cleaned, it was now my responsibility to make sure Margo took her tablets each day. There were thirteen different types and they had to be taken at different intervals. I had to keep an eye on her, make sure she did not set light to herself, or that she did not beat the living daylights out of my brother. I had to make sure that she did not mix the Valium tablets up with the Librium. Whilst other children were making sure that they kept their own rooms tidy, I was making sure that the whole house remained immaculate for my father. Surely there couldn't be any more responsibility for me to take on . . . or could there?

One day Shaun and I came home from school to find the front door wide open.

I went inside and called out to Margo, but she didn't answer. The bedroom door was wide open and the bed made. Her clothes were gone – there was no sign of her. My first thought was to run down the road and see if I could find her. I knew that I would be blamed for this. Unsure what to do, we both went to the breakfast room and waited.

Eventually, my father came home.

'Where's Margo?' he demanded.

Shaun and I shrugged our shoulders. My father went to the bedroom, and came back. He was holding a piece of paper.

'She's gone!' he said. 'This says that she can't cope with the family any more and that she's going away so she can get better!'

Around the same time, my best friend, Beverley, told me that she was moving away. She was so excited; to her, it was an adventure she was taking with her family. I was stunned – speechless. I thought we would be best friends for the rest of our lives. But once again, I was being left. First my mother, then Nan, Margo, and now, my best friend, Beverley.

My father began to cook for us. It was *always* curry. Actually, my father was always very strict about what Shaun and I could and could not eat. At school, we had to join different lines if bacon or ham were on the menu, and he always quizzed us when we came home. I remember him shouting at my nan one day because she gave me a bacon sandwich. I did not understand what was wrong with eating bacon and ham, although I knew it was something to do with my father's culture, where pigs were considered unclean animals.

He didn't speak much about his culture, but one day I came down for breakfast, and found him waiting for me. In his hand he held what looked like a box, covered in a green cloth. He handled it very reverently, with care and consideration. I had never seen him take care of anything before.

'Come and sit down, Shireen. I've got something I want to show you!'

I took my seat and he began to uncover what I thought was the box. To my surprise it was a big, thick, heavy book. He disappeared into the kitchen and washed his hands, face and his feet. Then he came and sat down beside me, opened the book and began to read. He told me that the book was the Koran, his holy book. I studied him carefully as he read the words, scanning each line with his fingers. He was different when he read this book. I sat still, not moving, whilst each word went straight over my head.

In these times when I had his undivided attention, all I wanted to do was ask every unanswered question that I had in my head. I missed my friend and I could not share that sadness with him; I missed my mother and I wanted to know why he had allowed her to go away. I missed my nan and I could not forgive him for treating her so badly. Now I was living in fear that what had happened to her would happen to me. I wanted to know where she was now. I never got the chance to say goodbye to her; I wanted to tell him about that, but I did not. Instead, I dutifully listened whilst he spoke out the contents of his book.

It made a change from my usual solitary reading – times when I would lock myself away and lose myself in a book, or even write poems. One day, during school assembly, I was given a little red Bible – a New Testament and Psalms – by an organisation called the Gideons. Stories were read from this book; stories about God. This, too, was a holy book, but it wasn't the same as my father's. I was told that the God in the little red book sent his Son to earth and that he died on a cross, bearing the punishment for humanity's sin. The stories I heard were so close to the fantasy world that I lived in that I readily accepted what I was being told. And I could identify with the suffering of this Jesus; after all, I knew about suffering. I knew what it meant to be beaten and bruised.

So I liked this little red book and began to read it for myself. I enjoyed the stories that were in it, so in order to keep it safe, I naturally hid it from my father. I often thought about the words in that book; there was a feeling of *love* about them. Something about that book made me feel strangely warm inside. The words he was reading from his holy book didn't appear to convey the same feelings of love; it was a puzzle. But for all the warm feelings that the little red Bible stirred up in me, cynicism and anger had built up a very good wall around me and I made sure no one got past it. I never allowed sentimental thoughts about my family to creep into my mind and I made sure that I never wished for anything, other than being free from this life. It was easier and far less painful to shut down and block out all happy memories of my mother and how she had been towards me as a small child. I could not afford the privilege of remembering the times of waiting for that bell to go, just to see her waiting in the school playground. My thoughts towards my mother now were totally bitter. I told that little girl that I used to be that no one wanted her and that it would be better for her to go away.

From the time my father introduced me to his holy book, I started to sense that he had begun to see me differently. I wasn't sure what that meant, but I felt uneasy. I began to find freedom in my cross country racing. I would drive myself to the very point of pain. I ran and ran and tried to escape the pain that was inside of me. I would feel the branches of trees hitting my face and legs but still I would drive myself. I would feel the rain on my face and coldness of the air – I felt alive. The beating of my heart and intensity of the adrenalin running through my veins made me feel on fire. Sometimes I would go off into my little world of fantasy and imagine that I was running towards my imaginary parents or into imaginary situations where I was the principal character and that other people were watching me because I was beautiful and wearing beautiful clothes.

I listened to my classmates talk about going shopping with their mothers or going out with their fathers and hoped they would not include me in their conversations. I never spoke about my mother or my sister and they never asked.

I started to win medals for cross country running and the attention that I received from my peers and teachers became the force that drove me harder.

Then, one day, Margo came back. But it wasn't a happy reunion. Her moods were becoming steadily more violent. She was so erratic – one moment she would be sane and rational, then without warning she became abusive.

This worked to our advantage, though, where our father was concerned. He seemed too distracted with her tantrums to bother with us. At night the arguing got louder and louder, until it would end up with Margo throwing furniture at him. He was sullen and moody but his bad temper was now aimed solely at her. They were forever arguing.

Still, at least it gave me some sort of reprieve – not one that lasted, though; it wasn't long before Margo had moved out again.

Chapter 6

My New Role

I made the most of my limited free time. I would study people, their mannerisms, and then copy them. Sometimes, I would pick up about five or six different movements and begin to walk or talk like that myself. I felt I had no identity of my own, so I had to take others.

I did love cross country and all other sports – to run was to feel free. But I hated the changing room and shower experience. Showering after PE was a nightmare. All the girls in my class were now developing and they would wear pretty, flowery underclothes. Me? I wore white vests and navy blue knickers, the regulation undergarments. My physical shape was changing and I did not know what to do about it or who to speak to; it was embarrassing. Nobody had talked to me about these changes.

Still, I was changing, my world was changing, and I had to somehow fit into it. Looking at the other girls made me realise that I needed to update what I wore.

One day, I found the nerve to ask what I had to ask.

'Dad, I need to buy some new underwear. Can I have some money to go to the shops?'

He looked at me. My heart lurched as it always did when I met his eye. I could feel my face flush. He looked me up and down and, instinctively, I folded my arms in front of me. He seemed to stare at me for ages, then got up and walked towards me. I flinched as he came nearer, but he simply picked up his front door keys and put some change in his pocket.

'Come on, then!'

What? I didn't want him coming with me!

'It's all right,' I said, 'I can go on Saturday – '

He ignored me. 'Let's go and get you fitted up.'

In town, we went to a store, and soon found the lingerie department.

'Can I help you, sir?' asked a young shop assistant, glancing from my father to me.

'My daughter needs to be fitted for some underwear. Can you sort her out?'

'Yes, of course.' The assistant whisked me behind a curtain.

I had to take my shirt and vest off. I felt very vulnerable in front of the assistant, but the thought of wearing adult undergarments filled me with excitement. I was now one step closer to being – and feeling like – an adult, just like all my classmates. The assistant took the necessary measurements, and then disappeared, returning after a few minutes with a handful of bras. They were all different colours, with flowers and bows and lace.

Through the gap in the curtain I could see my father waiting. I wished my mother were here so that I could share this experience with her, but she was not and I had to do it alone. Wearing the undergarments made me feel different; I was only thirteen, but suddenly I felt mature.

Fully dressed, I came out of the changing room. I noticed my father looking at me, and for a moment I saw something in his eyes that made me feel strange.

'How would you like to pay for these, sir?' asked the assistant. My father just kept staring at me. 'Sir?'

Abruptly he came to his senses. 'Cash.' He paid for the goods and we returned home.

At home, I put on a dainty bra which had tiny light blue flowers all over it. I stood and gazed in the mirror for ages. I was an adult!

I didn't hear my father come into the room and was startled when he appeared. I quickly tried to get my shirt back on as he came towards me. But there was something about him that was different. He was silent, and when he came close, I could see the same look in his eye that he'd had in the shop when I came out of the changing room.

'Don't put your shirt back on. I want to see what you've bought with my money.'

I frantically picked up the bag with the other garments inside and tried to show him those. But it was not those that he wanted to see. His eyes were fixed on me. He took the bag out of my hands and put it down on the bed. I suddenly felt very sick. Then he placed his hands on me. As he touched me, all my senses were being woken up and I was repulsed by the feelings. I was shaking from head to toe, whilst his hands continued to move and explore the item that I was wearing.

'Please let me get dressed now!' I stepped back, but the dressing table was directly behind me. 'Dad – *please*!'

He seemed to snap back into reality, realised what he was doing and turned and left the room.

I sat on the bed and sobbed. I'd wanted so much to be an adult and wear the same clothes that the girls in my school wore but now, after seeing his reaction, I wanted to go back to being six years old again.

I felt sick for the rest of the evening. I tried desperately to push the incident to the back of my mind but every time I looked at my father, I kept seeing an action replay of what had happened. Sick and repulsed, I went to my room. I dragged my nails over my arms; somehow the physical pain of my flesh being scraped from my arms felt better than the inner pain that I felt. I began to blame myself. If I had not been trying on the clothes this would have never happened.

A few weeks after that awful incident, Margo came back to the house. She offered no explanation of where she'd been, but walked in as if she had never been away. My father just seemed to accept her back and life resumed in much the same way as it had before she left. One night, shortly after her return, I passed my father's bedroom and the door was slightly open. I caught sight of them in bed together and he was touching her as he did me that terrible day. I felt a surge of anger, because in that moment I realised that if Margo had not left, I would not have had to fill her place with my father. After that, I felt such contempt for her that it took all my energy to be civil.

The tension between my father and I was deepening. He never looked me in the eyes after 'the incident'. Margo was too wrapped up in her own problems to notice, and soon she'd left us once again.

Shortly after she'd left, my father's manager from work telephoned; he, and my father's GP, were apparently concerned about my father's depression. Shaun and I were told that we should do everything we could to alleviate his suffering.

'What about *our* suffering?' I muttered.

The only purpose I served at home was to clean the house and make sure my father's shirts were ironed. I had to get the shopping and make sure Shaun was all right. I was the housekeeper and the mother to my brother. Now I had to 'alleviate my father's suffering' as well.

One night I lay in my bed, hoping that tiredness would soon take its toll, when I heard my father stirring.

I could hear his bed creaking. Then, I heard the foot-steps.

All of a sudden, my bedroom door opened. My heart began to race.

'What on earth is he doing? I haven't done anything wrong!' I said to myself.

I kept my eyes tightly shut in the hope that he would turn around and go out again. I could not think what he wanted. He came nearer to my bed and I could smell the faint aroma of aftershave and hear his breathing.

'Shireen, are you asleep?'

I lay frozen in my bed; then I felt his hand slip under my bedclothes.

He took my hand.

'Shireen, I'm lonely and I need company!'

Need. He needed me.

The words from my father's manager came flooding back in my mind. Obediently I got out of my bed and followed him. Quietly we went into his room. He got into his bed and pulled the sheet back, gesturing me to get in beside him. I was in a daze.

I slowly walked over to his bed. This was the place that had been reserved for Margo and before her, my mother. His voice was calm and pleasant. That 'nice' side of his personality – the side he often showed to his friends and even strangers – was being displayed for me now, but I did not understand why. As I lay beside him, I could hear him breathing, heavier and heavier, louder and louder, almost panting. The smell of his aftershave was stronger than ever and he was warm and clammy. Then his hands moved over my body again like they had that day in my room.

My heart was crashing against my ribs. I could not comprehend what was happening. Then I felt something stab at me; it was hurting but I could not move. Again and again this went on until eventually my father went limp, turned over and went to sleep. I left his room and went back to my room. I was shaking.

Next morning, I knew that what had happened was not a dream because my body ached all over. My ribs hurt every time I breathed and my back was sore where my father had been lying on top of me. I was sickened by the whole episode and the feelings that it had left me with. I could not speak to anyone about what happened, not my classmates, nor my brother.

This was not to be a 'one off' but the start of a string of similar events. Night time became horrific for me. I prayed to the God of my Gideons' Bible. Night after night I prayed with desperation that my father would fall asleep and that I would be spared the ordeal, but for me there was no relief. I began to think that any God, if he was really there, was a callous and cold-blooded God who enjoyed and endorsed my pain because I deserved it. The love I'd read about in that little red book clearly wasn't for me.

I tried to make sense of the situation by convincing myself that this was just another role that I had to fill in the absence of my mother and Margo; after all, I had been told that I had to alleviate my father's suffering; I had fulfilled the other roles, this just became another, like vacuuming and cleaning . . . I told myself that, but I knew in my heart this was different.

The most confusing part was my emotions. My father seemed to have the ability to switch something on in me that I did not like. Usually the only way I felt my father's hands was as he slapped or hit me, but now, the minute he touched me, my senses seemed to heighten. I desperately told myself that these feelings should not be allowed to emerge, but they did. My body seemed to be filled with tingling that was not unpleasant but I knew it wasn't *right*. I wanted to scream and push him off me, I wanted the feelings that were arising in me to stop, but they did not. I tried to switch off from what was happening. I felt so ashamed and guilty.

What was happening? My classmates never talked about this; why not? Did all girls have to do this with their fathers?

In the morning, I was always left with feelings of disgust and an aching body. I would scrub my body and try to forget the tingling sensation by scrubbing my flesh until it went bright red. The pain offered only temporary relief from the pain I felt inside. I hated myself for not being able to turn off the physical sensations that were running through my body, and for not having the courage to stop what was happening. But the thought of his anger always caused me to remain silent. This was my new role; I had to put up with it. I crept around silently at night in order not to wake my brother – I   didn't want him to know what was going on.

Then we had sex education lessons at school. I watched in horror as male and female anatomy was explained to me. I was told how a child is born to a mother and father and then grows to find a mate of her own and has sex with that person. I was never told that a child is born to their parents and the father then goes on to have sex with her.

All around me were the immature and naïve sniggers of my classmates. To them it was a world of discovery that they were to enter into at the right time and in the right situation but for me it was a world that had been forced upon me – by my own father.

My childhood, my innocence, had been totally stripped away. I hated my father for doing this to me.

Each night, I had to keep a silent vigil on the staircase waiting for my father's light to be turned out. Only when I heard the creak of the bed, which assured me that he was asleep, only then could I afford to catch up with some sleep. I had learnt to cat-nap but the sleep deprivation was badly affecting me. Finally, I could endure no more.

One evening, I was sitting on my bed and beside me was a brown paper bag. I opened it up with calm determination, and emptied the contents into my lap. That night, I put forty tablets into my mouth and gulped a mouthful of water. Then I got my coat and slowly made my way down the stairs, unaware that Shaun was behind me.

'Where are you going?' he whispered.

'I'm leaving, Shaun. This time, it's for good.'

'I'm coming with you. I'm not staying here on my own!'

I was so tired. I couldn't argue with him. 'All right,' I said.

He shut the door quietly behind us. I thought I was leaving for the last time. And I knew exactly where I was going to die.

Chapter 7

On a Mission

We got on a bus that would take us to our mother's house. I didn't tell Shaun what I had done.

The tablets started to take effect halfway through the journey and I began to feel dizzy and sick. The voices of the people around me were fading and I was becoming disorientated. But somehow, I made it to my mother's.

As my mother opened her front door, I fell down. I remember thinking her carpet was soft and warm. I crawled into her bathroom and threw up again and again until the tablets were all gone. I felt so miserable as I realised that once again I had failed. I had been cheated one more time.

My mother was asking me all sorts of questions but I gave no explanation. I desperately wanted to tell her the truth of my ordeal. I wanted to beg her to take me into her home. Then I wanted to hit her for leaving me so that I had to be her replacement. I wanted to throw all her fine china on the floor and smash it. I wanted to go into my sister's bedroom and rip up her nice clothes and cuddly toys. But I did none of those things. Instead, I quietly put on my coat and followed her to the car, resigned to going back to the house.

I went straight up to my bedroom when I arrived. I felt totally defeated. I have since heard it said that only cowards end their lives but I don't think that many people have ever reached a place of total hopelessness. I had reached that place; my ambition had been to meet with death. But apparently even death didn't want me.

The tablets were no longer in my system and my mind became clear again. I lay on my bed listening to the sound of my mother and father talking downstairs. I did not even bother to creep to the top of the stairs to hear what they were saying. After all, what could he say to her? He wouldn't tell her what he was doing to me, would he? I just lay there feeling hopeless, knowing that tomorrow would now be the same as all my yesterdays. When she left the house that night, I wasn't sorry to see my mother get into the car and go.

The butterflies that had been my long-time companions had changed into little demons, who spoke to me. They seemed to have a collective voice that whispered softly in my ear, reinforcing my hatred: 'Don't let down your guard . . . you'll only be hurt again. You have every reason to hate. You're *right* to hate.'

I grew to have no compassion, no mercy. I completely shut out the world and closed the door to everyone around me. I had nothing but contempt for the whole human race, and all I wanted was to be left alone by everyone.

However, I had to have a plan. If death wouldn't take me, how could I get out of my situation? I resolved to do well in school and get good qualifications – that seemed to be the only way I could escape my circumstances. I began to force myself to listen to the lessons and write notes as the teachers spoke. My hearing was still not good; much of what I heard was muffled, so I decided to swallow my pride and speak to my Head of Year to see if I could be moved nearer to the front of the class. She agreed. I had my chance. Now I had to focus myself, and succeed.

I still loved to be involved in sports. I had heard about the Surrey Championships through my PE teacher and decided that I wanted to give it a go. There was circuit training, trampolining and gymnastics, all of which I thoroughly enjoyed. PE was the one way that I could work off my frustration and get away from my home life. It had become more my refuge than my pastime.

I was thrilled when the team list for the championships was posted on the school notice-board and my name was there. That night, I lay in my bed and dreamt of going to the Olympic Games, and winning medals. I thought of touring the world and meeting famous people. Crowds were cheering me and throngs of people were throwing roses onto the track as I ran past the finishing line. They were applauding as I bent down to have the ribbons put around my neck. I was a winner . . .

As well as my running, I was fast becoming the class 'swot' because I was studying so hard. I didn't care what people thought, I was going to succeed. I was on a mission. And it was beginning to pay off.

My father noticed my dedication to my studies.

'Well,' he commented, sarcastically, 'looks like you might be good at something, for a change. Just as well. This running lark isn't going to pay the bills in later life. I'm glad to see that you've come to your senses!'

'I haven't come to my senses! I still like running and gymnastics but I've decided that if I want a decent career, where I can travel the world, I need qualifications!' I retorted.

'You won't have time to travel the world when you're married and start having kids of your own!'

'I'm not getting married, and I'm certainly not having kids. I want a life!' I shot back.

His voice rose. 'Oh, you mean you don't want the kind of life I got lumbered with, when your mother walked out on me!'

'You can't blame us for what your wife did to you!'

'You'll get married when I say you will!'

I knew I had to change the subject. Otherwise, it would have ended up with me taking a beating.

'If he thinks he can dictate to me how I will live my life when I get older, he can dream on! I'm not having him tell me what to do all my life. I can do what I like when I reach eighteen and there's not a thing he can do about it!' I said to myself, as I reached in to pull his wet shirts from the twin tub. I'd been washing his shirts and ironing his trousers since I was nine years old. Well, that wasn't going to be how I'd live when I was older. No way.

As well as class-work, I was training hard for the championships. One day, during the PE class, my friends and I were laughing, having fun. We'd got the trampoline out and it was directly underneath the parallel bars. Someone suggested we jumped on the trampoline and then somersaulted over the bars. I'm still not sure what happened, but I hit a bar with immense force. I crashed to the floor and lost consciousness soon after.

I came round in the ambulance. The sound of the siren was hurting my head. I put my hand up to feel my forehead and my fingers found the v-shape dent. It was deep. I started to cry.

At the hospital, I had to wait in the corridor, on a trolley, before I was wheeled into the X-ray department. There were various other people in the same area, also waiting to be X-rayed. I fought to stay awake. Then I felt myself being prodded, and was jolted into consciousness.

'What the hell are you doing, having the school phone me, telling me to come down here, eh?' Yes, it was Margo, who was back in our lives yet again. 'Haven't I got enough to worry about without you dragging me in here to look after you?'

The people who were waiting with me in the corridor looked on in amazement as this crazy woman began hitting me and punching me around the head. I tried to fend her off. The green hospital gown that had been put on me became loose and torn as she grappled with me. I felt sick, and my nose began to bleed. Two security men and a nurse came rushing over. The men tried to restrain Margo, but she kept breaking free.

In the end, they wheeled me away to a nearby examination area, and the nurse pulled the curtain around me to hide me from Margo.

'We've got rid of her, sweetheart,' said the nurse, comfortingly. 'What a terrible woman. I wonder who she was?'

'She's my stepmother!' I cried.

'What! You mean you actually live with that woman?'

'She's ill, she's schizophrenic!'

The next morning, I was told that I could go home once I had been seen by the doctor. I was in no hurry to leave; after all, I was only going back to him. But then I thought – what if Margo has to come and get me? Remembering what she was like the day before, I started to panic.

'OK, Shireen, we've spoken to your father,' said the doctor as he checked the dent in my forehead, 'and your mother is coming to get you. You can go as soon as she gets here!'

That afternoon I lay quietly on my mother's settee. She had given me a cream-coloured cardigan to keep me warm. I so much wanted to ask her to let me stay but my pride would not allow it. Instead, I went back to my father's house. There was no anxious parent waiting for me, no kisses of affection or loving hugs. I got no apology from Margo for her behaviour the day before. It was a flat, unfeeling welcome from flat, unfeeling people; nothing more than I expected. The only person happy to see me that evening, was my brother. Still – I had the Surrey Championships to look forward to. Only I didn't. Part of the training meant I had to go away for orienteering and my father would not let me go. He simply refused to let me take part. So that was that.

As I recovered my strength, I felt a grim determination within me. I had tried many ways to get out of my circumstances. I had run away and the police had brought me back. I had run to my mother's and she had taken me back. Twice I had tried to take my own life, but even that had failed. But I was absolutely determined that one way or another, I'd be rid of these people. I would do well in my exams. I would find a job and get a place of my own. Little did I know that plans had been made that would threaten to destroy that dream.

I knew my father was from another country but I'd never asked him about his family or exactly where he had come from. I never asked him about anything, and he never spoke about his family abroad. Then one evening, he announced that we were going on a journey to see his father, in Pakistan.

I was shocked. I didn't want to go there. Why would I want to meet his family? If his family were all like him, I certainly didn't want to know them. Another thought struck me.

'What about my revision? I've got my exams! I won't have time to do any on the trip! Can't I stay here?'

No. My father was adamant. We were going to Pakistan.

He and Margo started buying clothes for us and for members of his family. In the shops, he made me parade up and down in trousers and long dresses, whilst he looked at me. He would twirl me around and play the loving father in front of the shop assistants; he could play to his audience with all the charm of a politician. I felt disgusted, thinking that if they knew what he'd done to me, they wouldn't have laughed at his jokes so readily.

At school, there was a buzz of conversation about exams, leaving school and careers. But what about me? Here I was in this vacuum. My father was taking me to Pakistan when I needed to revise! He didn't want me to have a career; he did not want me to leave home. I didn't really know what he wanted me to do, except remain his unpaid housekeeper. I was going to take some books to Pakistan to revise for my exams, but still, I worried and feared for my future.

Chapter 8

Culture Shock

The morning of our departure soon arrived. I woke up with a sense of dread.

My clothes had been neatly laid out on the chair at the end of the bed. I got up and went straight to the bathroom, peering down the stairs to the suitcases, lined up in order of size. The doorbell rang, and in walked a friend of my father. He had come to the house several times, and was taking us to the airport. I had as little to do with him as I could. He and my father would often talk together in a foreign language, which made Margo angry because she couldn't understand what they were saying. Perhaps she felt threatened. I know I did, when they spoke together whilst looking over at me. Was my father telling his friend what he had been doing late at night?

The journey to the airport was long and silent. My father was continually speaking in the strange language that only he and his friend understood. I looked out of the window, trying to fight back the tears. To me, the next six weeks seemed like a prison sentence. But to my brother Shaun, this was an adventure – it got him out of school, and it was exciting.

The twenty-one hour flight was arduous. I stared out of the window for a long time, watching the clouds pass by. Then I looked around at the people on the plane and noticed how many of the women were dressed in brightly coloured fabric. They, too, were speaking in the language that my father had spoken to his friend. I glanced over at my father. I absolutely loathed him. I began to think of the times he tried to be nice to me – mainly when we were in the company of other people – but I never trusted those times. I marvelled that my father could appear to be such a proud man, a man of charisma and intelligence; and yet in my eyes he was a monster. And here I was on a journey to meet the people who had either turned him into the monster I believed him to be – or people who would be just the same as he was. Whatever I was about to be faced with, I knew I had to be ready.

The aircraft came to a slow halt on the tarmac of Karachi Airport, and Shaun reached up into the over-head compartment to get our bags down. He handed me mine. Inside that bag was everything I treasured from my life in England – my revision books, and my little red Bible. Yes, it was still with me, hidden away from my father's eyes – and hidden on this trip from those who would surely confiscate it. I still read it, still found some comfort in it . . . sometimes. At other times, I'd glance through it and then throw it against the wall in fury when I read about love and kindness; it hurt so much to read about something I had never known.

Outside the aircraft, the heat was unbelievable. I had never experienced anything like it. My clothes, which were appropriate in Croydon, now stuck to me. After we had waited for the rest of our luggage we went through to the main part of the airport, which was as busy and noisy as London's Heathrow – and yet, this was nothing like Heathrow. The women were dressed just like the women on the plane. They had lots of material wrapped around their bodies – saris – and coins sewn into the headdresses. The men wore tops and trousers that looked like pyjamas.

I watched as a man came towards us. He was wearing a white naval suit. His strides were long and confident. His buttons were very shiny and the stripes on his shoulders must have meant that he was a man of authority. His eyes were on my father. I thought we were in trouble – but we'd only landed an hour ago! What could we have done wrong?

Then the man's hand came out, and he shook my father's hand, greeting him with great affection. They spoke together for a few minutes, and then the man looked at us.

'This must be Margo,' said the man, graciously. 'It is a real pleasure to meet you. Did you have a good journey?' Then he looked at me, and smiled. 'You must be Shireen. When I found out you had been given that name, I was thrilled. It is a beautiful name, as is the person who bears it. I hope you will enjoy your stay here!' He put his arm around my shoulder, and then smiled at Shaun. 'And you, young man! You must be the handsome one of the family! Your father is nearly as good-looking as you are!'

My father turned to us. 'This is my cousin's father, my uncle,' my father told us. 'We are going to stay at the services club, where all the naval officers and army personnel are.'

We walked to an open-air car park, and there a man got out of a black limousine and opened the rear door. He was dressed in a dark suit, with a white shirt and dark tie. He bowed as I approached. Then he gestured to me and I got into the car, welcoming the coolness of the air inside.

The journey did not take long and soon we arrived at the place where we'd be staying for the next six weeks. The darkness of the windows in the limousine shut out the views of our surroundings as we drove up, but once I stepped outside, I was able to see the full beauty of the trees and different coloured flowers that filled the air with such fragrant scents. The building we were to stay in stood tall and impressive compared to the buildings around it; its plush interior was filled with leather chairs and ornately carved wood which gave it a very majestic feel. It was like being in a palace. There were huge tapestries hanging on the walls. This was nothing like Croydon, or anything I had ever seen in England. This was a new culture and a new way of life entirely.

My mind slipped back to the time that my father had tried to teach me the Koran. Maybe he was trying to tell me about this part of his life, and that was why he had read that book to me.

We were shown to a large room which had a very high ceiling. It was very ornate. There were three beds, neatly made, complete with mosquito nets. We were all going to be sleeping in the one room.

After we had settled in, our clothes unpacked, and we had washed ourselves in our marble bathroom – the taps, shower and mirror were all inlaid with gold, as were the legs of the bath – we made our way to the restaurant downstairs. The coolness of the room was inviting. We made our way over to the centre of the room and sat at a table, not saying a word to each other. A woman dressed in a brightly-coloured sari came towards us, holding a pad and pen. Her hands were covered in intricately designed brown squiggles, all over her fingers and over her palms too. My father tried to impress us as he spoke to her, in her language – which we discovered was Urdu – seducing her with his wit and charm, whilst we sat in dumb silence. I smirked as I looked at Margo's face, which was turning red with anger.

'Do you have to speak in that language in front of us?' she spat at him as soon as the waitress was out of sight. 'It makes us look stupid!'

My father glanced around the room. He looked embarrassed as she shouted at him.

'Keep your voice down!' he told her.

'Well, how are we supposed to know what you're saying? You could be saying anything, couldn't you?' Margo went on.

I watched them arguing as it sank in – I had to spend six weeks non-stop with these people.

A man approached the table. Before we knew it, my father shook the man's hand and entered into conversation, those foreign words pouring from their mouths. They laughed and hugged each other, whilst all we could do was watch until my father finally acknowledged our existence and introduced us. I dutifully stood up and shook the man's hand, he bowed as he took mine, then turned and said something in Urdu to my father, and they both laughed. I dragged my hand away and sat down, refusing to make any further attempt to converse. How dare they, I thought to myself.

That evening, the same car that had brought us from the airport came to pick us up from the hotel. It took us to the house of my father's uncle, where we were to have dinner.

We stepped out of the limousine and walked into a garden area. There was a fountain, and many unfamiliar flowers. The scent of jasmine and honeysuckle filled the air. The inside of the house was spectacular. Dark brown tiles covered the huge entrance hall; they gleamed in the sunlight. All the walls were covered with ornate carpets with pictures of men and women in the local dress. Huge fans with carved blades, suspended from the ceiling, wafted cold air around the room, making it pleasant to sit in. We were led into a huge sitting-room, with sofas and large matching cushions. Gold ornaments were littered about on shelves that were made out of onyx and black marble.

My father's uncle left the room, then without warning a crowd of people came bursting in. They ran towards my father first, grabbing his face and kissing him. The women were crying and the men were shouting, as they patted my father lovingly on the back. The noise was deafening. Shaun and I looked at each other. We had never seen such a display of emotion like this before.

The group then turned their attention to Margo, Shaun and me. I stared at my father. He was actually *crying*.

'Shireen, this is your grandfather!' he mumbled.

I looked at the elderly man in front of me. He shakily but tenderly took my hand.

'How do you do?' I said, timidly.

He turned and shook Margo's hand, then Shaun's.

'And this is your grandmother!' my father said. I gazed at the frail old woman, dressed in a sari, who stood no more than four foot tall.

The introductions went on for at least twenty minutes. Aunt after aunt, uncle after uncle, and lots and lots of cousins . . . It was too much for me to take in. I was seeing members of *my* family; people I had never known. These were people who were related to me by birth; they had the same blood as me, but I had never heard about them before. In all the years I had lived with my father, he had never once mentioned his father or his five brothers and their families, and yet here they were, eager to get to know me and my brother. I was overwhelmed with curiosity. These were people who, unlike my father, wanted to know everything about me; my likes and dislikes, my desires and dreams and my hopes for the future! I had a natural mistrust of all of them, but they seemed quite genuine. But *why* were they so interested in me, when I had never heard of any of them? There couldn't be anything sinister behind their interest – could there?

Chapter 9

Beautiful Princess

I woke up to the sounds of this foreign country. I looked out of the window and watched droning motorbikes weaving in and out of oncoming traffic, their engines straining as they carried entire families. Horses clopped along, pulling brightly coloured rickshaws. I wasn't used to the sun shining brightly as it did first thing in the morning. At home, it would not be this hot until mid-afternoon at the height of summer.

The noise that was going on in the street matched the noise going on in my head. Memories of the night before, all the people I'd met . . . I had so many questions.

A knock at the door interrupted my thoughts.

'Come in!' My father shouted from the bathroom.

A man came in pushing a trolley laden with food and tea. He nodded his head and left, silently. I began to feel hungry as I looked at the toast and marmalade and omelette.

'I'm starving!' exclaimed Shaun.

'You don't know what starving means,' muttered my father. 'You'll get to see it whilst we're here – believe me.'

Margo sat quietly, black mascara smudged around her eyes. She was just about coherent; her medication hadn't taken effect yet. I looked at my father, wanting to ask about the family we had met the night before, but somehow I just couldn't. I picked up the pot of tea and began to pour it into my cup. Beige, sweet-smelling liquid came out of the spout – not what I was expecting.

'What on earth – ' I began to say, when my father cut in.

'They make tea with hot condensed milk here. It's not like at home. If you don't like it, leave it. Don't make a fuss!' He took the pot from me and poured some in his own cup, as if to convince me that it was all right to drink.

I took a bite of omelette. Immediately, my mouth felt as if it was on fire, and I grabbed a pitcher of water. The innocent-looking dish of eggs was laced with tiny shavings of chilli peppers! My father snatched the pitcher from my hand leaving me drenched with water.

'What are you doing?' he yelled. 'You don't drink any water that doesn't come from a bottle, otherwise you will be violently sick!'

'How was she supposed to know?' Margo said. I was amazed, hearing her stand up for me.

We were picked up by the limousine that morning and taken to a market area, where the driver spoke to my father and then left. The streets were dusty and there was an all-pervading smell of rotting fish. Stalls lined the streets in the market-place, much as they did in Croydon, but this was so different. Fabrics of all different colours were the main item, broken up by barrows which displayed onyx jars and elephants, black onyx cigarette boxes and ashtrays and other local wares. There were rugs of every description. The shops that were hidden by the stalls showed off their herbs and spices; chillies and cooked food were displayed in metal containers. This was a sight I had never seen before accompanied by smells that I had never smelled before. We were led to what looked like a shop doorway, which was broken in places and covered in chipped green paint. The wooden stairs were cracked and broken; in fact, some had broken in half, leaving a very dark, narrow, precarious staircase. Unable to see properly, I went up, disorientated by my surroundings. Everything about this journey had left me puzzled. Climbing this staircase was no exception, as I wondered what would meet me at the top.

We came to a room, which was stark and shabbily decorated. The walls were covered in a greyish-coloured plaster, apparently having had no form of decoration on them since the time they were constructed. There were no pictures, only a couple of old settees in the middle of the room. There was a window seat covered in cushions, and rugs were scattered on the cold, grey stone floor. At the far end was an alcove with a single-ringed burner. An elderly woman was sitting cross-legged in front of it on the floor, stirring a pot.

'That is my mother's mother!' My father told me, as he watched me looking at her. My grandfather was there, too. He came and hugged me so tightly that I could feel his bones under the thin layer of his parched, dry skin, which hung like paper over his shoulders and back.

My grandfather spoke to me, but I was unable to understand him. My father interpreted. Another woman appeared, carrying a pot. I noticed that her hands were covered in the same intricate brown detail as those of the waitress the day before. As she came closer, I could see her face. Her eyes were beautiful, framed with black kohl eyeliner which made them look even more almond-shaped than they already were. She had a diamond in her nose and ears that were highly decorated with all different kinds of earrings.

'This is my brother's wife, your aunt, and this is my brother, your uncle,' said my father.

The woman nodded and smiled at us. She wore no shoes but her feet were covered with a gold ankle bracelet that had what looked like gold chain mail attached to it. This covered the top part of her foot. It tapered off and was held by a ring on her big toe. Silently, she faded into the background, making no conversation.

My grandfather beckoned us to come and sit by him on the settees. He hugged Shaun and me so hard that we couldn't move. Eventually, he released his grip and we moved away to the window seat. Margo tried hard not to look bored.

The women of the family remained very much in the background, the only evidence that they even existed being the smell of cooking that was getting stronger and stronger. Shaun and I gazed out of the window at the passers-by. Then my father spoke to me.

'Shireen, you go through to the back. Margo, Shaun and I will remain here for lunch.'

'Why do I have to go through to the back?' I asked, indignantly.

'Because that is your place and that is where you will remain, until I tell you otherwise!'

My grandfather stood up, visibly upset by my father's harsh tone, and quickly came to put his arm around me, scolding his son as he did so. My father glared, came over and gripped me tightly by the arm – enough to hurt me, but hiding what he was doing so the others wouldn't see. He spoke to me in a low voice.

'You will not disrespect me in front of my family, do you hear?'

I went and sat down with the two women in the alcove. I was unable to converse with them and didn't know why my aunt had stroked my hand and face. I assumed it was to reassure me. She held out a metal bowl and spooned in some meat and gravy, along with diced potatoes; then she handed me a round flat pancake, known as a chapatti. I was feeling too hot to eat anything but did not want to offend my relatives, so I accepted the bowl. I waited for a knife and fork, but none came. My aunt made an eating gesture, as if to encourage me that this is what I should do.

'What do I eat with?' I asked her, forgetting she could not understand.

Straight away, my father was on the scene. He was still angry at me.

'They don't have knives and forks here. They eat with their hands! Watch me!' He snatched the chapatti out of my hand. He broke a piece off and held it between his thumb and index finger, then he scooped up some of the meaty gravy, with a potato in the middle, and ate it. Twice, I tried to imitate him and twice, I ended up getting gravy all down my clothes. He began to get very agitated.

'Can't you do anything, you idiot?'

His father came running and began to shout at him in Urdu. It sounded like my grandfather was standing up for me. My father stood silent, whilst my grandfather pushed him and raised his hand to him. I had never seen anyone raise their hand to my father. I was shocked. My grandfather then came over to me and put his arm around me, stroking my face with love and affection. I could feel his heartbeat racing with anger towards his son. I smiled inside. My grandfather's actions had reminded me of Nan. After that, my father was careful never to flare up at me whilst in the presence of his father.

The temperature rose by several degrees that afternoon and my great-grandmother beckoned me to take a sleep on one of the beds that I'd seen in the back part of the room. I lay down obediently and watched as my great-grandmother put a mosquito net around the bed. I soon fell asleep, as did everyone else. When I woke up I had to go to the bathroom. I asked my father very tentatively where it was. He pointed to a door that had once been painted white, but through the heat, the paint had flaked off and most of the wooden slats had fallen out. Behind it was a dingy, empty space with grimy whitewashed walls and a dirty rotting plastic container, filled with water. On the floor, grooves had been cut and in between them there was a hole, which I assumed was a plug-hole. The hole in the wall – a window had once filled the space – looked out onto the veranda of the next-door neighbour's flat. I glanced up to see a man walking past. He was staring at me.

'What on earth do I do now? Where's the toilet?' I said to myself.

The length of time that I spent in that room must have been an indication that all was not well because my aunt came to see if I was all right. Seeing me standing by the door she must have sensed my apprehension. She gently pulled me aside, stepped inside the room and crouched down. Then she dipped her hands in the plastic container to show that it was for washing hands. I was horrified! No toilet paper, no chain to flush! I came out of that place determined never to take my toilet at home for granted again – and to always remember to carry a whole lot of toilet roll with me wherever I went whilst in this country.

Later, I was introduced to a boy of my own age. His name was Ali. He was my uncle's son. He was very good-looking, a head taller than me. He had a moustache and spoke very good English. He took me to a local park when the sun went down and it was cool enough to go out.

'Shireen, there is something you must understand,' Ali said. 'Whilst you are here, when we are out in public, women walk three steps behind the man, at all times. You must have your head covered, and you must never speak to a man first – he must speak to you. Will you remember this?'

'Er . . . I think so!' I said, not really understanding.

My father had not told me about the difference between east and west. I had not been told about the protocol that had to be observed in this country. Things that I took for granted back home did not apply here. I could not wear what I wanted here, nor could I sit in the presence of men like I did back in England. I had to learn about the restrictions, and Ali educated me accordingly. He reached into his pocket and pulled out a long, lilac silk scarf, which he carefully draped around my head.

'There, you look like a princess!' he said, with a warm smile.

We walked along by a pool that had been made to run the full length of the park. The grass was immaculately kept, with almost every blade of grass seeming to be the same length as the others. The trees were full of bright orange flowers with a delicate fragrance. Ali walked alongside my brother; then, as if willing to break with protocol, he came alongside me.

'I thought you were not allowed to walk with me?' I said.

'No, but you are foreigners, so it will seem as though I am narrating our history to you and informing you of your surrounding area.' He grinned. 'That would be seen as acceptable behaviour!'

The way he spoke and the words he used puzzled me. I had noticed that his vocabulary was unlike mine. He used a broad range of words which you would find in a dictionary but were not used in the everyday language

of the west. We may have been from the same family, but
his home was thousands of miles away from mine, and
his ways were thousands of times different to mine. So,
not only was I faced with a language barrier but I was
faced with a huge cultural barrier, too.

I noticed how good Ali was with his younger sisters –
so caring. As we walked, they came running over to us,
and it was interesting to see how he treated them. One
of the girls had all but lost her headscarf; Ali picked it
up, put it over her head and tenderly smoothed down
her hair.

'I must make sure they observe protocol in public,' he
said to me.

'Shireen, do you know the man that you will marry?'
asked one of his sisters.

'Sorry, what do you mean?' I said, taken aback.

'Do you know the man that has been set aside for you
to marry, when you come of age?'

'I don't have a man set aside for me to marry,' I
replied, a little puzzled. 'And in any case, I will only
marry the man that I choose, not one that has been chosen for me.'

Ali pulled his sister aside and spoke to her in Urdu. I
sensed that she was embarrassed by what she had said.

'Shireen, I am sorry. I forgot that you are being
brought up in England and that the ways of our two
countries are very different!' she said, humbly.

As if to change the subject, Ali said: 'Shireen, did you
know that your name is an ancient Persian name – the
name of a deity? Not only are you regarded by the family
as very special because you are the firstborn, but you carry
a very important name that is not often heard of any more.'

I didn't know how to reply to that.

I lay in my bed that night, staring up at the white
mosquito net. The conversations I had had with my

cousin had made it difficult for my brain to switch off. Somehow, here in this country, I felt different. I felt like I belonged, even though because of my half-English heritage, my skin was not the same colour as that of my relatives. These people had a special place in their hearts for me even though they had never seen me before. I was important to them and even though we could not freely converse, they conveyed their love in their own way. I had watched as my grandfather stood up to my father, which was something I had not seen since my nan was alive. My attitude was beginning to change and I could feel myself really warming to these people. I was confused by this amount of affection, not daring to believe that it was for real, but it did *seem* real.

The next day, we were taken once again to my grandfather's house above the market in Bondi Street. My aunt came to meet us and spoke to my father in Urdu. They spoke so fast and in so much depth, I thought something had happened.

'Your aunt wants to take you to get you a couple of saris, and some other bits and pieces. I said you'd go!' My father told me, dismissively.

My aunt took me by the hand and led me to the market. We walked beside the rows of stalls until she stopped at one that was filled with rolls and rolls of brightly coloured fabrics. There were cottons, silks and linens of all different shades and textures. My aunt seemed to know the man on the stall and talked with him. He held up all sorts of different material in a dazzling array of colours as my aunt shook her head or nodded. I just stood by silently, not able to understand what they were saying but leaving any decisions to my aunt – who had the money. Assorted headscarves were brought out, and then the stallholder pulled out a tape measure and measured me for a top, known as a *choli*, which matched the fabric my aunt had purchased. My aunt seemed very sure of what she was doing, and took her time in choosing just the right things for me.

In the end the choices were finally made. We walked away from the stall, armed with fabric for saris and *cholis*, and *salwar kameez*, the pyjama-type suits they wore, and headscarves; my aunt had even bought me lots of coloured bangles to match my new outfits.

My great-grandmother grabbed hold of me as I came through the door. All the men were there, including Ali and his brother. Shaun and Margo were sitting amongst them, looking bored. My father stood up and began to talk to my aunt in Urdu. Then reached into his back pocket and took out a wad of notes. My grandfather stood up too and, although I could not make out what they were saying, it looked like my grandfather was telling my father off. I smiled as I watched, enjoying the spectacle of seeing my father being brought down a peg or two. Then my uncle got up and began to reassure my father. I could still hear raised voices as I was ushered into the back room. My great-grandmother began to undress me, which made me feel very self-conscious. When I tried to pull away, she put her hands on my face and kissed me on the forehead. Her fingers were all gnarled and the bones were misshapen. Her hands shook as she tried to unzip my jeans and undo my shirt. Eventually my aunt took over and the process was speeded up. My great-grandmother stood holding the fabric, waiting patiently in the background as I put the top on. Then together, my great-grandmother and my aunt began to wind the fabric around my body. It was blue and was speckled with gold sunbursts. On and on the fabric went. Then the sari was complete.

My great-grandmother reached up and put a red bindi spot on my forehead. She sat me down again and reached for my hand. Then she started to draw intricate lacy detail all over my hands, and my aunt carefully painted the outline of my eyes with black kohl eyeliner.

Once they were satisfied with the finished product, they led me into the main room where the voices were still raised. My father took one look at me and his jaw fell. Then my grandfather turned to look at me, put his hands up to his face and began to cry uncontrollably. Everybody else, including my brother, stared at me in stunned silence.

I must look awful, I thought to myself.

I looked to my aunt for reassurance. She must have seen how hesitant I was because she smiled, as if to say that everything was all right. My grandfather came over and showered me with kiss after kiss, still crying.

'You look absolutely beautiful!' Ali said, beaming from ear to ear.

'Why is Grandfather crying then?' I asked.

'He thinks you look more beautiful in our customary dress than you do in your western clothing. He is right. You will make a beautiful bride one day!' Ali smiled.

Both of my uncles were still sitting in stunned silence, whilst my father looked at me in amazement. I couldn't tell if he liked me in what I was wearing or not; I didn't care. The other men obviously did like it. For once in my life, I was the centre of attention and felt elated. The moments that they spent looking appreciatively at me seemed to last forever and I loved it. Margo just glared, hating to see that all eyes were focused on me. And I remembered what my cousin had called me – a princess. At that moment, I truly felt like one.

Chapter 10

Uncle Yaqub

That afternoon, we were to take a trip to Hyderabad where we were to meet with another of our uncles, who was in the army. The journey was to take about ten hours, and we would be travelling mostly over dry, dusty desert land. I stared out of the limousine and saw flat, desolate terrain. With that kind of view, and the close proximity of my father and Margo, I decided there was only one thing to do – sleep.

I was woken up by the feeling of my brother jamming his finger into my arm.

'Wake up. We're here!'

We stepped out of the car into unbearable heat. We were met by a man who looked like a thinner version of my father. He was quite distinguished with a moustache and was wearing a green army uniform with a beret, neatly folded in two and held by a buttoned strap to his shoulder. He was crying as he ran down the front steps of the house. This was our uncle.

He grabbed my father with such brute force that he managed to sweep him off his feet by a couple of inches. Margo, Shaun and I watched and waited – we were getting used to this sort of greeting.

'This is Margo, Shireen and Shaun,' my father said, after a while.

'Margo, it is lovely to see you! I hear such good reports on how you make my brother so happy!' my uncle said, enthusiastically.

Shaun and I looked at each and fought to contain our laughter. Our father glared at us – that made us stop sniggering.

'Shaun, what a handsome and strapping lad you are! I imagine that you make your father proud, always!' My uncle went on, patting my brother on the head and then turning to me. 'Shireen, I hold my breath in amazement at how lovely you are, like a lily, full and blooming as when the midday sun shines on it!'

'Eh? Oh . . . thanks,' I muttered, as he bent down to kiss my hand.

'My name is Yaqub,' said my uncle.

He beckoned us inside the house, where we met his wife, who bowed her head silently and held out a jug of lemon tea – it had lemons floating on top. The coldness of the air inside was refreshing, because we had been standing for a long time in the mid-day sun.

We went into a dining-room. The table and chairs were very ornately decorated, with carved legs and onyx inlays. The table was inlaid with gold filigree. The smell of the food that was laid out, like a banquet, was mouth-watering. My uncle had pulled my chair out from the table, in order for me to sit down, much to the disgust of Margo, who had to pull her own chair out. This amused my brother immensely, causing my father to smack him on the back of the head.

'We have not been blessed with children yet. But I hope, one day, to have two lovely children just like yours!' my uncle said to my father.

I raised my eyes as I ate, to see my father's reaction. There was none.

I loved the attention I received from my uncle. The attention I got from him – and my grandfather, other uncles and cousins – was more than I had ever had at home. My uncle Yaqub really seemed to like me. I noticed that Margo and my father were not amused by his attentions. I encouraged him all the more, bordering on flirtation.

Later, in the cool of the evening, we were taken by a car to see the changing of the guard at the mausoleum of Quaid-i-Azam Mohammad Ali Jinnah. As we began to climb the steps, we were confronted by a huge crowd of beggars. They came from all directions, their faces bearing the marks of poverty and their skin hanging as a result of it. I was horrified as I looked at the dirty faces of children and babies who had limbs missing, men who had no eyes and women who had huge boils or warts on their faces and hands. One man's legs were so badly deformed that they were in the shape of a dog's hind legs. My stomach turned as I tried not to stare. They clawed at us, some holding the hem of my garments and others grasping my wrists, as I desperately tried to hold onto my clothing. My uncle fought his way over to me. With one arm around my waist and the other holding the crowd at bay, he managed to steer me away from them.

'Alms for Allah, alms for Allah!' they shouted.

Suddenly, men wearing the same khaki green uniform as my uncle came towards us brandishing huge rifles. The poverty-stricken men and women were refusing to let us go, but the threat of the guns seemed to deter them. The crowd dispersed, and we continued to ascend the steps to the tomb.

Inside, everything was plated in gold. The mosaic ceiling glistened with rubies, emeralds and other precious stones. There were men sitting on their haunches, rocking back and forth, reciting things out of similar books to the one my father had read to me; this was their holy book, the Koran. As I looked around I saw a coffin, inlaid with the same stones as the ceiling, and surrounded by golden railings. I was told that the railings were there to stop people from stealing the jewels. Knowing what was outside of the heavy gold doors, I could not help wondering why there was so much poverty out there and so much obvious wealth in here . . . with the dead.

My uncle came over to me and placed a handful of coins in the palm of my hand.

'These are for you, my sweet. Now that we have made our sacrifice to Allah, and said our prayers, we can give to the poor. Hand these out to them as they converge on you again, and do not worry, for I will watch over you!'

We left the tomb and stood on the steps as the changing of the guard took place. The sound of their boots as they marched in unison echoed into the night. They held their formation with regimental precision, and the crowds who watched them looked on in admiration.

Once the ceremony was over, chaos ensued and once again we were overwhelmed by the same poor people as before. I held my arms up in the air and children jumped to grab the money from my hands. Eventually, when they saw that my hands were empty, they left. I watched from the top of the steps as they slowly descended, disappearing like a wave that had hit the shore and was now ebbing back, clutching the few coins that would save them from another night with an empty belly. And I remembered what my father had said to my brother: 'You don't know what starving means!' He was right.

As we walked back to the car, there seemed to be an argument between my uncle and my father. My uncle was throwing his hands in the air and smacking his forehead.

'Shireen! Shaun!' called my father, sternly. 'I want to show you something!'

We had to walk fast to keep up with his strides as he marched past the car. The houses on the main road stopped as he turned the corner. Here, the road turned to mud. We trudged through it and came to a place where sheets of corrugated metal had been crudely fixed together to form shacks. Rain from the night before had caused what little drainage there was to overflow and dirty little rivers ran down the road to meet us. The smell was stomach-churning. As we looked, we saw pathetic faces that were as grey as the corrugated metal, staring out at us with huge, sad, black eyes. Our clothes advertised that we had money, and many of the people saw this as a prime opportunity to beg from us – but the sight of my uncle in his army uniform kept them at arm's length. As we carried on down the street, we came across a cow lying in the middle of it, its stomach bloat-ed and legs rigid; it had been dead for quite a while. Its ribs were sticking out and flies gathered around its mouth, searching for debris from its last meal. I heaved and ran to the nearest sheet of corrugated metal . . . then I realised that this was housing maybe ten or eleven members of a family, and respectfully declined to expel the contents of my stomach all over their home.

We sat in silence as we made the journey back that night. My uncle attempted to speak to us about our 'shanty town' experience, but we had seen another side of life that we had never known existed until we had come here and it was a huge shock. The images of those poverty-stricken people were to haunt me for a very long time to come. I had rubbed shoulders with men, women and children, who did not know when they would have their next meal, or if the rain that came in the night would completely wash away their homes.

Back in Croydon, I may have had only coarse blankets to cover me at night, but at least I had a bed to sleep on. I thought of the times that I had envied my sister's fluffy bedroom, and realised that the harsh reality of what I had seen that evening had given me the ability to never want what she had, ever again.

This was a journey of discovery for me, and in some ways, I was grateful to my father for showing it to me because I *needed* to know that there were people on this planet who struggled and strived even to live. There was no place for pride in *this* world. Dignity had no room to manoeuvre in the lives of these people. Their destinies had been etched out before them in the form of corrugated cells, held together only by rusty nails. For them, the hope of a brighter future, and the ability to escape their world of pain would never come. I looked at the girls, who were forced to live in these grim and dirty surroundings and wondered if they, like me, were forced to fulfil the roles that I had to fulfil.

Something happened to me that evening that was to change my perception of life forever. I had grown to be cynical and suspicious of all people. I'd grown to hate more than I'd grown to love. The circumstances of my life and the things that had been forced upon me from such a young age had shaped the way that I viewed everyone. The people who should have been showing me love and nurturing me were the very people who were destroying me. But that night, I had witnessed people who were more unfortunate than I was, and I began to realise that they had even more reason to hate life. And strangely, the person who had robbed me of so much, the person who had never shown me love and compassionate feeling was the very person who had helped me to begin to *feel*, by bringing me to this place – my father.

For the rest of the time I was there, the memory of that shanty town never left me, but on a personal level, for me, Karachi was simply paradise compared to what we had left behind. This whole experience of meeting people whom I had never been told about and visiting places that I had never dreamt about was totally overwhelming. These people – my relatives – were treating me like I was a princess. They showered me with love. They had opened their lives to me and let me into their hearts. The affection that they were lavishing on me was so far removed from the abuse that I had suffered at the hands of my father that I hardly knew what to do. I was not used to affection and I did not know how to receive it without mistrusting it. The nagging doubt remained; were these people sincere in how they felt towards me?

One afternoon, we headed over to a relative's house to be guests at the wedding of his niece. The house was buzzing with activity when we arrived. Servants were running to and fro with garments that had been freshly pressed. Beautiful flowers were all over the house, and the heavy scent of jasmine and honeysuckle lingered in every room. I noticed that only the women were in the house, there were no men.

'Your aunts will be here shortly to meet with you!' my father said as he left the house.

Margo and I sat in the empty lounge and looked uncomfortably at each other. Neither of us knew what was going on. I had never been to a wedding in my own country, let alone a wedding in a foreign place. My curiosity got the better of me as I heard all the hustle and bustle going on in the background, so I got up to investigate, leaving Margo alone.

I went up the stairs and looked around. There was a door open to one of the rooms, and inside was a double bed, covered in red satin sheets. Rose petals covered the bed and a canopy of orange organza had been erected. Candles had been placed all around the room and a plate of fresh fruit sat on a table beside the bed, along with a jug and two glasses. The noise of chattering women became louder, and as I turned round a woman, dressed in orange and covered in coins and beads came towards me. She was the bride. Her hands and feet had been painted with henna in the now-familiar intricate design, and bangles covered the length of her forearms. Another woman appeared.

'Ah, beautiful Shireen, come! I have a beautiful sari for you to wear to the wedding! We must have photos of you wearing the costume of our country, you look delightful in it! Come!'

She took me to another bedroom, and there she found a white silky material covered with gold embroidery and teardrop-shaped mirrored beads. She clapped her hands and two women came running into the room. She spoke in Urdu to them, and they kept bowing.

I felt very nervous as the women fussed around me. I was uncomfortable, standing only in my underwear. Familiar feelings of vulnerability began to sweep over me – I wanted to run, but I couldn't, just as I couldn't run away from my father . . . all I could do was stand and fight back the tears. One of the women produced a jar that was filled with oil that had a very pleasant fragrance. The two women covered their hands in it and began to smooth it over my arms and legs. Their hands worked methodically and with equal pressure, driving the oil into every pore of my limbs. One woman took some more oil and reached to cover my torso, at which point my hand reached out to stop her. The women looked at each other, very embarrassed and unaware of what they had done to offend me. I tried to break through the language barrier and apologise; they

couldn't understand. Eventually I allowed them to continue and I gritted my teeth as they smoothed the oil into
the top half of my body, as I desperately tried to shut off
all feelings of disgust. I heaved a sigh of relief when they
had finished and continued to stand still as they took a
cloth mitten and buffed my body down with talcum
powder. Every muscle, bone and ligament had been
woken up by the constant working of their hands, and
now tingled as my body absorbed the sweet-smelling
oil.

The women then got to work assembling the sari.
Layer upon layer of fabric was folded with precision. At
long last they were satisfied and walked around me,
smiling in approval. Then, they sat me down and
applied make-up and the same red bindi spot that the
ladies all around me possessed. They led me downstairs
to the garden where all the women had gathered together for the wedding breakfast. My uncle's wife caught
sight of me and gasped in amazement as she threw her
hands up to her face. I caught sight of one of Ali's sisters
in the crowd, who also stood still and looked at me,
smiling.

Margo was in the far corner with a white shawl
around her head. No preparation seemed to have been
made to get her ready for the wedding. Her pale com-
plexion looked insipid against the white of the cloth. I
knew this whole experience was too much for her; all
she wanted to do was crawl into a bed somewhere and
hide. Suddenly, I felt panic-stricken. I could not remember whether she had taken her medication that morning.

'Margo, are you OK?' I said, really concerned.

'Get away from me!' she snapped.

I could see her eyes were red but was unable to do
anything about it for fear that she would start screaming
as she did at home. My attention was so fixed on her that

I had not realised that the crowd of women were coming towards me and sweeping me along with them into the front of the house. I felt my elbow being tweaked. It was Ali's sister.

'You look beautiful, Shireen! Wait till Ali sees you. Grandfather will cry also, you wait!'

'Do you really think so? Am I really pretty? Why do these clothes make me feel different to the clothes I wear at home?' I said.

'Maybe it is because you are free to wear these clothes here and they are an enhancement to your beauty, whereas your western clothes are a hindrance both to your body and your beauty.'

I had no idea what was about to happen. The crowd of women fell silent as the sound of music and drums began to get louder and louder. Around the corner of the street came two highly decorated wagons, pulled by horses, followed by a throng of men. Each wagon carried a throne made out of gold and embellished with flower garlands. On one of the wagons was a man dressed in a white silk *salwar kameez*; he had flowered garlands around his neck. The bride was sitting on the throne of the other wagon. They came to a halt outside the house.

During the ceremony, I looked around to see if Shaun or my father were there. They were – they were sitting with the other men on the other side of the room. I watched, unable to understand what was happening or what was being said. At the end of the ceremony, the bride and groom walked down a catwalk, and men and women were rushing to the front, pinning money onto their clothes. When they got to the end, the bride and groom were covered in paper money; huge wads were placed in their hands, as they thanked their guests for coming.

That night a wedding banquet had been put on for the guests. Meat and fish dishes were displayed in huge metal containers. Chapattis piled high on platters sat in the middle of the table and there were fresh vegetables and flowers. Wonderful aromas filled the house. I was simply overawed.

Every experience of this journey was opening me up to a whole new culture. I had never heard anything about this way of life from my father. All my life I had grown up with a feeling of not belonging. I knew that I was not wanted. But here I was being welcomed into the hearts and homes of loving people, so alien to me in culture and background, but so *accepting*. By now I felt secure in the knowledge of their love for me, which confused me even more.

I looked up and saw my grandfather coming towards me. Walking beside him was my uncle Yaqub.

'Shireen, I have just arrived for a three-day leave to join the wedding party of my cousin. I saw you across the room. You look the most beautiful woman in the whole of the room. Doesn't she, Father?'

My grandfather placed a very shaky hand on my cheek.

'You look like a lotus blossom coming into full bloom, my precious granddaughter!'

My uncle took my hand and placed it in the bend of his arm, and proudly paraded me around the room. I could feel the eyes of strangers staring at me.

'Shireen!' It was one of my female relatives. 'We have prepared an English dish especially for you. Our food may be a little too strong for your digestive system to take.'

I was whisked away to a table where my brother was standing, shovelling mashed potato into his mouth.

''Ere, sis! This tastes good!'

We both took our plates and went into the drawing room, where all the other teenagers were. I sat down next to Ali, who took my plate as I smoothed my sari down.

'Are you enjoying yourself, Shireen?' asked Ali.

'Yes, but it's odd, you know. My father never speaks to me about all of this. In England, there's just me and my brother. I hear all my school friends talk about their cousins and aunts and uncles and I just assumed I was alone.' And I told him all about my nan. 'And now,' I finished, 'my father brings me to the other side of the world and I meet all of you. I keep thinking I'll wake up back in Croydon and this will just be a dream and something that never really existed.'

'You are special, Shireen. You have the choice of embracing whichever culture you choose.' Ali smiled at me, and I thought he seemed a little sad. 'We have no choice; our paths are set and our futures decided by our fathers and forefathers. Our brides and husbands are chosen from the cradle and promised before we take our first steps. We are expected to live the way of our forefathers, regardless of individual choice. You live in the west. You have a choice.'

It seemed strange to hear that. 'Well,' I said, 'I have to work hard to pass my exams with good grades so I can make a good choice when I leave school . . . ' If my father doesn't stop me from doing what I want to do, I thought.

The next three days were spent with my uncle Yaqub, whilst he was on leave from the army. He looked smaller in civilian clothes, less official and more casual. We went to a beach called Hawks Bay. Margo wore a turquoise swimming costume and fell asleep in the sun, turning her back to a deep lobster red.

The day after our visit to the beach and my uncle's last day with us before returning to his rank, I became ill.

The food and the heat proved to be too much for me. I was vomiting so much that my body was going into convulsions. All I could do was lie on the bathroom floor, soaked in sweat. My temperature was rising by the minute and both my uncles and my grandfather were worried about dehydration. Every time I emerged from the bathroom I was a bit weaker. Margo, with her sunburn, stayed in the shower most of that day, dousing herself with cold water to help calm her angry flesh. Eventually, my father called on yet another uncle who was a doctor in the navy. He examined me.

'She has many mosquito bites on her body, and she is extremely dehydrated. I think she may have a form of malaria. She seems disorientated.' He glanced at Margo rather disdainfully. 'Put this cream on the back of that woman and her sunburn should calm down in a few days. It was a bit stupid to wear nothing but a bathing costume in this heat, wasn't it?'

My uncle Yaqub sat on the bed, with my head in his lap. I lay still; my ribs ached and my throat hurt, due to the endless retching. My uncle kept placing cool cloths on my forehead to bring my temperature down. I babbled on in my delirium.

Almost all the family came to see me whilst I made a recovery, which was slow. They left at night and then returned the next day. Then on the third day, I was able to keep a few sips of water down. Sip by sip, I felt stronger so that I was soon able to sit on the balcony with my family. My uncle had made a telephone call to his unit which allowed him to prolong his visit by two days, in order to be with me. He said he wanted to make sure that I made a full recovery before returning.

Before he returned to his unit, and when I was able to travel a short distance, my uncle took me to a jewellers shop, where he bought me a gold ring in the shape of a pyramid, with a filigree design all over it. It was a lovely ring, and so big that I kept getting it caught on my clothing.

We drove to the airport to see him off. He was back in his uniform and carrying a huge brown sack over his shoulder. His shoes clicked along the ground as he walked towards the plane. Army personnel were able to walk onto the tarmac with members of their family to see them off. The noise of the engines screeching just behind my ear made it impossible to hear what my uncle was saying, but I knew that through his tears, he was saying 'goodbye'. I watched his mouth moving, but was unable to determine what he was saying. I was continually brushing the hair and the scarf out of my face; it was being whipped up crazily because of the wind. The dust was going into my eyes and, in all honesty, all I wanted to do was get back to the car. But I could see that this was a traumatic time for my uncle. As he hugged me, I could feel the wetness from his tears on my cheek; then he turned and followed the rest of his unit up the ramp and within seconds, he was gone.

This man had treated me more like his daughter than my own father did. A part of me was very sad to see him go that day. It felt strange, knowing that there was a man in the world who loved me and was going into battle with my picture in his breast pocket, close to his heart. He had been proud to walk around a crowded room with me on his arm. He had diligently sat with me during my weakest hour and he had even bought me a gold ring to signify his affection. Hatred and love . . . abandonment and acceptance . . . poverty and wealth . . . I couldn't really take it in. But one thing I knew for sure: as I watched his plane soar into the sky, I had a feeling I'd never see my uncle Yaqub again.

Chapter 11

Goodbye to My Other Life

We were now into the fourth week of our visit to Karachi. I had seen sights and sounds that I had not even dreamt about in England. I had visited people whom I had never been told about and I had eaten meals that I had never seen cooked at home. Everything was alien to me – but I liked it. I had now lost quite a bit of weight as I was unable to tolerate most of the food. My brother was enjoying the trip immensely and was not looking forward to going back to England – and school. I was being kept so busy that I had not even glanced at my revision books.

The culture of this land was not familiar to me and yet, I was somehow a part of it. I racked my brains to try to remember anything my father might have said in the past about this place and these people, but my memory came up with nothing. I felt at times that something was at war inside of me and it was nothing to do with the little voice that whispered negative thoughts into my head. It was as if there was some part of me that had been woken up, a part that really identified with this way of life. I had read things in my Gideons' New Testament – things about poverty, about an ancient way of life – which I was now *seeing* for the first time. I had seen women drawing water from a well, beggars lying at the temple steps, and I had been through a desert.

The way of life out here had a kind of romance to it with the seductive aroma of cooking and the fragrance of flowers. Perhaps, I thought, this way of life would seem dull and lifeless to westerners; the pace would be considered too slow and mundane. And what we thought of as 'poverty' didn't even begin to touch what I'd seen and witnessed here: children born into ghettos and mud slides whose fate lay in the hands of their parents; parents whose only choice would be to maim those children from infancy, in order to reap the few coins that would be enough to buy them one more meal; men and women who had the same grey pallor as their surroundings, with dirt ingrained into their skins, harsh calluses on their hands and feet as they scoured the dumps for anything that would bring them a few meagre rupees . . . The western culture would never see poverty on this scale. To these people, the western culture was summed up in the lives of movie stars and rock bands; lots of money, and endless parties. I knew that our relations would certainly be awestruck by the life we lived in England. Would they see a shallow existence? I didn't know; even if they did, they certainly wouldn't comment. These were humble, caring people who thought nothing of giving up their last meal to a stranger.

The years had certainly hardened my heart towards people. I had no reason to care about anybody, because no one cared about me, but this journey was, in a sense, my salvation. In Pakistan, I learned to open myself up to people again, to trust them and not hold them at arm's length. I had travelled four thousand miles to learn to live again.

I reflected on these points as I lay on my bed writing my postcards.

'Sis!' my brother called to me in a quiet voice.

'Yes?'

He moved over to me. 'Why do you think that Dad never told us about any of this? Do you think he was ashamed, or something, like he is of us?'

'I don't know. Only he knows the answer to that,' I replied. 'I can't see anything to be ashamed about though, can you? Anyway, these people are a whole lot nicer than he is. I wonder what *did* make him come to England and leave all this behind?'

And, of course, soon *I'd* be leaving 'all this' behind, too. But the trip had really given me a love of travelling. I loved boats and planes and any vessel that was used to carry people from one place to another, one life to another. When I was back in Croydon, I would dream of places where I could go and feel safe and of great worth to someone; I used to imagine I could escape to such a place, as I watched the trains pass by my house. Amazingly, my dreams had become a reality. I was in a place where I was being loved and cared about, there *were* people who loved and accepted me. Part of me was west – but part of me belonged in the east. I was living in a world where the two cultures could not have been any more different, but it felt like the divide was becoming less and less as the days went by, even though I had only been here for a short while.

But wouldn't you know it? The life-changing trip didn't end well for me. A little while before we were due to leave, we were visiting a harbour to see the aircraft, and I was so engrossed in my thoughts that I did not see a pothole in the road as I walked along. I felt the sharp pain shoot through my foot and heard the breaking of a bone. I screamed. My father came running towards me, as did Margo and Shaun. I slumped onto the road, trying to lift my foot out of the hole; it had swollen to twice its normal size and I could not move it for the pain. The break was now obvious to see. I had to go to hospital.

I was very nervous, remembering what had happened when Margo came to the hospital in England that time. As I waited, I expected my father to start shouting at me, but it never came. In fact he was showing genuine concern, which amazed me.

After my foot had been X-rayed, it was then plastered. The doctor gestured me to stand, unable to communicate with me, and he explained to my father that I was to walk on my toes. He said there would be no need for crutches after a few days when the pain had worn off. Armed with painkillers and crutches, we left.

'How do you do it, sis?' asked my brother. 'You get a fever, a broken foot – '

I didn't bother to answer him.

We went to my grandfather's house, and of course I had to climb the stairs. I eventually reached the top, exhausted by struggling to make my way up the broken and hazardous stairway, with my crutches. My grandfather looked horrified when he saw me. He started crying again as he smothered me in kisses and stoked my hair with concern. Then he let me sit down, realising how tired I was.

'I wish he wouldn't cry every time he sees me!' I whispered to my brother.

'It's only because he's concerned about you, sis!'

'I know, but I can see Dad's face glaring at me. I bet he thinks I'm doing it all on purpose. Anyway, Granddad keeps having a go at him for not making a fuss of me, doesn't he? Surely he must see how much he hates me, everybody else can!'

Shaun gazed at my father and my grandfather, sitting together on a settee. 'I think he just thinks that Dad has changed a lot being in the western world. Dad's ways aren't Granddad's ways any more. Maybe Granddad doesn't understand him and that's put a distance between them,' my brother said, thoughtfully.

'You know, you're really growing up!' I told him, surprised at his maturity.

The next evening, all the family went to a nice restaurant. My grandfather and grandmother were there, with my father's brother and his wife, and my cousins.

The air was thick with the now-familiar scent of jasmine and honeysuckle. Candles were lit, and were placed in bottles that were caked in dried candle wax. The tables were covered with white damask cloths and elegant napkins. We sat down and within a second waiters came, hurrying and scurrying around us, putting plates and chapatti bread on the table.

A band was playing European songs, and I felt an unexpected pang of homesickness. To take my mind off things at home, I allowed myself to get caught up in the music. I began to sing; I hadn't realised that I was singing so loudly and that everyone's attention was on me, until my brother nudged me.

'Shireen, why don't you sing up on the stage?' Ali asked.

'Oh, no, I'm sorry, I didn't realise . . . I apologise!' I said, rather shocked by what had happened. But they insisted. They wanted me to get up and sing.

I looked over to my father who nodded, as if to say that it was OK. The next moment my uncle had gone up to the band and asked them if they would be willing to accompany me, and they agreed. My heart started to pound as I looked at the people sitting at their tables, enjoying their meals.

Ali eagerly escorted me up to the stage. The band spoke English so it was easy to speak with them. I asked them if they knew the tune to *Memories*, and they did, and within minutes, they broke into the most beautiful melody. Embarrassingly, I missed the first entrance.

A thought slipped into my mind. I remembered something. It was something I had read in that little New Testament. The book said that if I asked God for help then he would do it. I needed help right then, in front of all these people. Strangely, I found that I wanted to do something that would make my father proud of me! I desperately did not want to seem like a failure in front of him. Confusing emotions . . . I had to pray.

'Dear God, please help me.'

As I opened my mouth to sing, I felt a surge of electricity run right through me. It was as if I was being lifted off the ground and taken to a higher place; peace flowed right through me. I held every note and remembered every sentence of the song and enjoyed every single moment of it. For the first time in my life I had a confidence that simply had not been there before. The sound of the applause and shouts of commendation filled the whole place; my family were standing as they applauded – *even my father*. Then I was called to sing another song, which I did. It was a night to remember.

My uncle Yaqub, was with his regiment, in the thick of battle. He had sent me a letter telling me about everything that was happening in his life. I was quite shocked to face the reality that the man who carried a photograph of me in the breast pocket of his uniform was on the battlefield and facing death. He had spoken to me about Allah before going away, but I wasn't interested. I had decided long before, when I was twelve, that if there was any God at all, it was the God who was spoken about in my New Testament. I had heard the words of the Koran and I had read the words of the Bible and made my decision, even though I was often angry at this God who allowed me to suffer so much – even though his Word spoke of love.

And yet, here was this man, a Muslim who believed the words of the Koran, prepared to take the life of another, writing words to me, his niece, whom he had only known for a short while – words that spoke so passionately about love. He even addressed the letter to 'My most loving *daughter* Shireen'. My father had never portrayed such love and had never spoken to me the way that this man did, and yet he followed the same book. I just couldn't understand it; the same blood flowed through their veins, and yet my father was nothing like my uncle. Even my grandfather was different to my father. I could not understand why so much anger and hatred flowed through my father when nothing but peace and love flowed through the members of his own family.

I read Yaqub's letter, captivated by the words on this piece of paper. He had written me a poem, as he lay in his barracks. And he had done as he said in the poem. He had signed his name in blood. I could not draw my eyes away from the letter. I retreated into my thoughts and tried to work out why this man had sent it. I was a fifteen-year-old girl, whose childhood had been denied her, who had been robbed of her innocence, leaving her in a world of washing clothes and looking after her brother and schizophrenic stepmother. Responsibility had been thrust on me at such an early age, stripping me of any idea of love and tenderness. I had only known a world of abuse and intolerance. How was I supposed to respond to Yaqub's letter? And yet, I didn't doubt he meant those words. I had found it difficult to put aside my shield of cynicism because a small part of me wanted to believe that humankind was not as bad as it had been portrayed to me through my mother and father. I *wanted* to believe that someone did see something in me that was worth shedding his blood for. I had read about a man in the New Testament who had apparently done the same thing – for me. He had seen something in this dark, meaningless world that caused him to shed his own blood. The Bible said he was the Son of God and that he loved me. So why had I suffered so much?

I had very little time to myself, but what I had, I grabbed. I woke up at five o'clock the next morning with the sun shining on my face and the breeze gently wafting the mosquito net. I got dressed quickly and quietly, leaving everyone else asleep. I made my way – clumsily, because of the plaster cast – down the marble stairs to the garden.

I struggled over to an ornately-decorated folly that housed some wicker chairs which overflowed with colourful cushions. There I took out my New Testament and studied the words, desperately trying to gain some spiritual insight. I needed to know why I felt the way I did; this intoxicating emotion that the letter seemed to evoke in me. I kept looking at the letter and gazing at the squiggles that made up the name 'Yaqub' written in his own blood and reading with fascination words of love that had never been expressed in this way to me before. I felt a warmth wash over me, as I began to realise that I really was worth something to somebody. The expressions of this man, put down on paper, astonished me and conflicted with everything else that had happened in my life. I was determined not to be swept away by such words, just as I was determined not to be swept along by the words that I read in my Bible. They were nice words, sure, but I wasn't a 'Christian'. I wasn't about to surrender my life to anyone or anything.

As time began to pick up pace towards our departure, the conflict inside of me began to pick up as well. It went round and round in my head: *here* I had recognition and was actually *loved*, but what was to meet me when I went back to Croydon? Would I be slaving away again for a man who demanded I share his bed when Margo was unable to satisfy him? Would I be doing that by night, and cooking and cleaning for him by day, shouldering the responsibility of my brother and Margo, as I always had?

My father had made it clear to me that I would never be able to leave home and pursue a career that led me to different countries. I hadn't wanted to leave Croydon and come here, but now I found myself wondering if I actually wanted to go back to all that I knew to be familiar. I had changed since I had arrived; here I felt like I had some form of identity. Here I did not have to make up stories of a life with a fictitious family and imaginary friends; here, I was held in high esteem and loved by family and friends. But there was no way out; our visit here was coming to an end, and the visits to our family were becoming more sombre occasions as they began to prepare for our departure. My grandfather seemed to be constantly crying and hugging us. Ali and the others were trying to spend as much time with us as possible when they came home from school in the afternoon. They took us to a local fairground, to parks, where we strolled and talked for ages. We would sit on the benches and enjoy the cool, scented evening air. I felt that I would never smell this smell again. Anyway, we made every moment count, and those last days weren't without excitement.

One day, shortly before we were due to leave, I was watching my father and brother looking through postcards we had collected during our stay. We had gathered pictures of mausoleums and hotels as well as keeping some of the small change as a reminder of our holiday.

Margo was very quiet. I felt she resented me all the more during this holiday, perhaps because of all the attention I was receiving.

I made my way slowly over to the balcony of our room to see if the man who regularly flew his eagle from the balcony next door, was flying the magnificent bird that morning. It was something I had grown to enjoy watching every day, and the man who flew the bird had even allowed my brother and me to feed the eagle titbits of salt beef. We were fascinated by the eagle; it had a bell around its foot, which tinkled when it moved. The brown downy hair on its head was smooth and glossy, as were its feathers; we could tell the eagle was well looked after.

'He is very tame,' his owner had told us. 'I have had him since he was small. He had hurt his wing and he cannot go back to the wild any more. He is too domesticated!'

That morning, I waited and then I heard the familiar screeching of the bird. The eagle was proud and handsome. He had the sharpest of stares. His eyes pierced into me, as if he could read my thoughts.

'I'll be going soon,' I murmured. 'I'm going to miss you.'

The bird soared up into the sky, a symbol of freedom. I wished I was that free.

After breakfast, my father took us all to Empress Market, which was the place to do souvenir shopping. I was dressed in the local clothes, whilst my brother and Margo wore their usual western clothes. Even my father wore western gear. They walked and I hobbled along, looking at the stalls, gazing at the local wares of onyx and ornaments. We passed men and women sitting cross-legged on the ground in front of metal bowls filled with spices and herbs, turmeric and curry powder. Fruit and vegetable stalls, alive with flies buzzing around them, were a great attraction. We continued to pass through narrow alleyways and came to a corner where two streets merged together. On the corner was a coffee hut; men were sitting at the tables with jugs of water and cups of coffee in front of them. They were passing the time of day with each other in their local language. I wished I could understand Urdu; I had missed so much by not being able to converse with the people here in their own language. For example, I knew my grandfather came from Goa in India, and had made his home in Karachi after living for a time in Hyderabad; I wished I knew more of his background . . . *my* background.

I was aware of the men at the coffee hut staring at me. I felt so self-conscious that I did not see the rather large wicker basket on one of the tables, and I knocked it to the ground. The lid flew off and rolled away.

'Oh, I am sorry – ' I began. But the men sitting around that table jumped up quickly, with such frightened expressions that I was stunned into silence.

My father looked around to see what had happened and came running towards me, looking equally frightened.

'Stand still, Shireen, and do not move!' he shouted as he ran.

'What have I done?' I said.

Everything had gone quiet and then I heard a rustling. Very slowly I turned and saw a hooded cobra. He had reached nearly a foot in height and was staring at me, his forked tongue flicking in and out. I was terrified. His tail was vibrating violently; he was getting ready to attack. The frightened men circled the snake, whilst one held a canvas potato sack outstretched. I decided to focus on my father, who was gesturing me to stay very still. This allowed the man with the sack to draw nearer to the cobra, undetected. In an instant, he threw the sack over the snake, and pulled at the drawstring. Then he safely released the snake back into the basket and firmly slammed the lid down.

My father came over to me, not shouting but holding out his hand as if he knew that I had become frozen with fear. We immediately went into the enclosed market area, which was nicely air-conditioned – and at that point, after my brush with death, I really needed to feel that coolness. Much later, when I thought about that episode, it seemed as if my father had cared what happened to me at that point. It was very strange.

Our final night came and we had to pack to come home. A big meal was laid on and all our family turned up, and although everyone was sad that our visit had come to an end, we had a good time.

'Shireen, I hope that we may see each other again some day,' said Ali, as he held my hand. 'I have had a most pleasant time whilst you have been with us, I hate that it must come to an end!'

'Ali, I want to say thank you for taking care of me and explaining your ways to me,' I said. 'I never in a million years thought I was part of anything like this. It's been completely mind blowing, all these people, my family!'

'Will you write to me when you get back to England, or will you forget me?' Ali asked.

'Ali, I will write to you,' I promised. Then I added, 'But maybe not for a while, because I will be doing my exams as soon as I go back.'

The journey to the airport was a solemn one. We were now in our drab western clothes and our suitcases were packed to overflowing with our eastern clothes and ornaments and jewellery that we had bought or been given. As we travelled, I gazed out at the country that had opened up so much for me – a country I wasn't sure I would see ever again.

My grandfather was unaware that he was holding my hand so tightly that he was nearly cutting off the circulation in my hand, until I began to wiggle it about. Then he realised, quickly putting my hand to his mouth and kissing away the pain. I watched the scenery change from the tree-lined streets, smelling of jasmine and Chinese roses, with the local people slowly meandering along with their metal lunch baskets in their hands, to the grey, muddy-looking shanty towns, filled with equally grey-coloured individuals picking through the rubble on their doorsteps, to the huge sky-scraper buildings, rising to meet the eastern sky. Then we arrived at the airport. Our holiday was over. We boarded the aircraft.

Two worlds had collided, east and west, and I had one foot in each. The blood and the culture of the land that I was now leaving had lain dormant within me. I never knew of its existence until now. These people were my people and yet they were strangers. They had treated me like royalty and had longed for my arrival into their lives, whilst I knew nothing of them or their existence. They had shown me a love and an acceptance that was from their hearts, even though they had never set eyes on me before. Now, I had to leave it all behind. My heart was heavy as I watched the land below become smaller until it fitted perfectly within the confines of a window that was no bigger than a porthole. Eventually, I could see nothing but clouds, and my 'other life' was gone.

Chapter 12

In the Park

I sat and watched the trains thundering past. Thoughts came rushing into my head of times when I was a child and wished that I were on one of them and that it was taking me to another life.

I had spent my young life escaping to a fantasy world where I was loved and cared about, but most of all, where I belonged. Now, a curtain had been pulled back, like in the theatre, revealing a play that had taken place thousands of miles away. The people playing the roles in this play wore strange clothes and spoke a strange language. They were from another culture, and in this play they had welcomed me into their lives and homes and loved me unconditionally. The role that I had been used to playing in England was not needed in this play. In that play, I didn't need to be a mother to my brother, a nursemaid to my schizophrenic stepmother and a wife to my father. Those roles I knew all too well. But now, I had been introduced to another role, the role of someone born outside of that culture and lifestyle, but who nevertheless had a part to play in it. This was a real life role where I was wanted by these people and they saw me as important.

I had never simply been a daughter or granddaughter and I found the new role refreshing and satisfying. For a while, I was loved – I was a princess. But now the curtain had closed again, and that part of my life was gone. I felt I would never have another chance to experience it again. And I began to think that instead of being something that counted in his favour, this journey of revelation actually had to be the cruellest thing that my father could have done to me.

My mind was now filled with a whole lot of new questions. I was trying to understand where I fitted in and what world I was really a part of. My roots were most obviously in the culture of my father. But I had grown up in a western world, integrated into a western society, which was much more liberal than the one that I had just left behind. In their world there were strict rules and regulations that seemed strange and restrictive to me, but to my relatives, were just something that they took for granted and lived by. It was a way of life that came as naturally to them as running did to me. But one thing that I did notice was that the women were happy and content, living, in a sense, *behind* the men, who offered them love, respect and protection. I envied them that.

My father had taken everything, my childhood, my adolescence. He had even robbed me of my identity and a chance of knowing that I had a family somewhere in the world that cared about me – something I was a part of. Their culture may have been worlds away from the one that I had always known, but they certainly knew how to love. I was left with a sense of fulfilment when my grandfather loved me and hugged me, but my father was the only one who felt any sense of fulfilment when he had 'loved' me. All I was left with was a sense of disgust and shame as I was left to sneak back to my room, like some shady mistress in the night. I hated waking up in my bed the morning after, gouging my skin till it bled. I was filled with loathing after my father had filled me with *his* brand of loving.

My relatives in Pakistan knew how to make me feel like I belonged. That was something that I had tasted and seen that was good. How, now that I knew all that, did I pick up the pieces of my western life?

The first day back in Croydon was spent unglamorously at the local hospital, having my foot X-rayed and re-plastered. The doctor had informed my father that the foot had been plastered at the wrong angle and that within a few months the bone would break again. They put a bandage on it to give it support and I left the hospital.

The journey back home with my father was a quiet one. We never spoke about anything of importance anyway; I informed him of any relevant details about my life that he had to know about, but that was it.

I tried desperately to camouflage all thoughts and images of the last two months. I threw myself into my schoolwork with a very real determination to do well in my exams and get decent qualifications; but it was no good, Pakistan had left its mark. I had tried to concentrate on the revision set by my teachers, in order to catch up for my exams, but I had been far too distracted by my exotic and exciting new life. Now, my mind was being kept alive by the letters that my uncle sent to me from his army unit. They were all filled with words of love. He spoke endlessly of his time with us and how his life was now complete, now that he knew the part of his family that he had always prayed for but never actually seen. He said he kept my picture in his wallet and took it out every time he wrote to me, and told me that his army 'chums' were very jealous of him.

As predicted, twelve weeks after the cast had been taken off, the bone broke under the pressure of kicking a football on the playing fields at school. Once again, I was on my way back to the hospital, and once again, my foot was in plaster. I was seen by a very good-looking doctor. He picked my foot up and examined it carefully, all the while not taking any actual notice of *me*.

'Hmm . . . we'll take an X-ray of your foot to see if there any other breaks and then we will have to plaster it again for you.' He then asked, in an unemotional voice: 'Are you pregnant?' I was shocked. Why would he ask me such a question? My father had now joined us in the room where the plaster was being put on. He stood silently in the corner. When the doctor had finished dealing with me, he shook my father's hand.

The next morning, I woke with absolutely no energy for my exams. My little butterflies, or demons, or whatever they were, fluttered about in my stomach, churning up waves of fear. I felt quite light-headed as I made my way to the bathroom. Getting dressed was really difficult – I had to get my clothes over the cumbersome plaster-cast (which was thigh high). Eventually, I managed to dress and left the house with no words of 'good luck' or 'hope it all goes well'.

The next six weeks were hard. Even getting to school was difficult, and left me little energy for the exams. I was so glad when they finished that I hardly had time to worry about how well I had done; just getting through them was enough.

My sixteenth birthday had come and gone with no real celebration, but that and the end of my exams marked the end of an era. Childhood really was now officially over.

My father had put a stop to all plans that I had made regarding some sort of exciting career. I had signed up for the Wrens but he would not give his permission for me to live away from home. I enrolled in the Royal College of Nursing and had been accepted, but again, he would not allow me to go – he didn't want me to live in the dorms of the college. He put a block on everything. Yet, when my exam results came through and he saw how poorly I had done, I took a beating like never before.

Not so long ago I had been living in a world of care, but now again I felt so trapped in this world of misery that my father had created. The emptiness inside me just kept growing.

I still had the daily chores of washing and ironing, whilst keeping an eye on my brother, who I noticed was becoming more and more hostile. He was beginning to have a very real problem with anger. His face would sometimes contort into such a rage that I feared that he and my father would come to blows. I felt under such pressure to get him to calm down, but the more I tried, the angrier he got. I understood why he felt that way; I knew that he behaved as he did because he had to fight the same battles each day as I did. His relationship with our father was one of hatred, too, and it did not help that my stepmother continually told him how much like his father he was. My sense of duty towards him began to grow even stronger, but I felt helpless to deal with him; I no longer had the ability to bring peace into his life now that he was getting older. As hard as I tried, I could not quell the raging storm within him.

I was now allowed out of the house during the day. I was still a solitary person. After my chores were done, I would visit the park and daydream about what was to come. It was the same park where I had tried to end my life but, somehow, it offered the friendly familiarity that I needed, even though the memory of what happened there still haunted me. I would take my books and sit on the grass under a tree, listening to the trains rushing by. Hours would pass and I would people-watch as office workers would come and eat their lunches; I'd watch as families would come, laughing, enjoying themselves, bringing their picnics. Day after day my routine never changed.

One day, I was so engrossed in my book – and with my thoughts – that I did not realise that someone had come to sit down just yards away from me. I looked up and he was just sitting, staring at me. Then he smiled and made his way over to me.

'I've been sat here for ages just watching you. I like the way you smile when you read something funny in your book. You were totally unaware of me!' he said, in a friendly manner.

At first, I was unsure about him. He was an extremely good-looking man. He had dark hair and deep blue eyes and spoke in a deep gritty voice with a slight accent. But I did not welcome the interruption, regardless of how handsome he was.

'I'm sorry. Would you like me to move to some other part of the field?' I asked, hoping that he would get the hint.

'No, not at all . . . Look, I just saw you and felt attracted to you, but if you would like to be alone with your book, then I will leave!' he said, not unpleasantly.

I didn't know how to reply. I no longer knew how to read people, and I had very little experience of men other than my father and his friends.

He laughed. 'I can see that you would rather be alone, so I will leave you in peace. Hopefully I will see you again!' He was obviously not put off by my lack of interest.

The next few days, without fail, he was there. I knew in my heart that he was coming to the park to simply see me, even though I showed no interest towards him. I told no one about my 'admirer'. But it was becoming increasingly difficult to ignore him, as he persistently sat within yards of me until in the end I had no choice but to acknowledge him.

'My name is Marco. I come from Tuscany in Italy and my family have bought a restaurant here.' He named a road. 'You may well have seen it!'

'Yes, I think I have.'

'What is your name?'

'Shireen. I live . . . er – just around the corner!' I was not going to be caught off guard. He might have started turning up at the house, if I had told him precisely where I lived.

He kept on coming to the park and talking to me. I started to think about him when I was at home. He told me that he was twenty-three years old and I could not understand what he saw in me. I was only sixteen. Still, he seemed genuinely keen to see me and so we began to arrange to meet more frequently in the park. He would bring a bottle of wine and some Italian biscuits and we would sit and talk for hours. I told him that he was not the first man I had met from another country. I told him about my family in Pakistan, and he seemed to find that most interesting.

Marco spoke with the same elaborate diction that my family had spoken with in Pakistan. He used long and descriptive words to explain his way of life and the culture that he had been brought up in. He confided in me – he said he was finding that adapting to the way of life in England was very difficult. After my experiences of adapting to a new way of life in Pakistan, I fully understood what he meant. For a while, I felt awkward in his presence but in a very short time – only three weeks – I had got used to him and began to really enjoy his company.

The early warning bells that were ringing when we first met, had now ceased and I now felt good about being with him.

One day, Marco met me in the park as usual. I saw that he did not have any wine or biscuits this time; that struck me as odd.

'Shireen,' he said, reaching out to take my hand, 'would you like to come and see the new house that we have bought? It is not far. I am very excited about it. Why don't you come and give me your opinion about it? It would mean a lot to me.'

'Oh, I don't think that's possible!' I said, as I tried to pull my hand away. But he tightened his grip and I noticed his face began to change. His expression was becoming more and more intense. There was a strange look in his eye . . . then something must have snapped him out of his thoughts because he loosened his grip and smiled.

'I'm sorry, Shireen. Because I am on my own so much I forget that I must not offend you . . . but I enjoy your company and want very much that you should see my new home.' His blue eyes were pleading. 'Shireen, please say that you will come!'

I looked at him, and said, 'Well, all right,' in a very reluctant voice. And against my better judgement, I went with him.

He had promised to get me back to the park by five o'clock. We walked down to the restaurant that his family owned. He spoke to five men of similar age to him whilst I stood behind him. I started to feel very vulnerable – and then they laughed with each other. The feelings of unease intensified.

'Marco, I think I've changed my mind. I would like to come with you another day, but not today. Is that OK?' I asked.

'You must come with me *today*. I insist!' he said, smiling.

As we drove past familiar sights in Croydon, I began to get more and more apprehensive about the whole situation. My heart began to thump as all the familiar places faded away and places and buildings and streets I didn't know took their place.

At that point, I panicked. Frantically, I shouted at Marco to stop the van so that I could get out. That was when he leaned over me and pushed the door lock down. Then he held my arm so tight that I could not move. I was in deep trouble and I knew it.

Chapter 13

Ordeal

I began to cry. I could not break free of Marco's hold. Then he spoke to me through clenched teeth.

'I *told* you that it had to be today that you saw my new house, didn't I?' His eyes blazed with anger.

We arrived at his house and I knew that my fate was in his hands. He was about a foot taller than me and much stronger. My heart was still thumping and my mouth was going dry as the heel of his hand drove me up to the front door. I looked around to see if I could call out to anyone, but the street was deserted.

I was led upstairs to a room that was furnished only with a bed; there were no sheets or blankets. Feelings of terror rose within me; feelings that usually surfaced every time my father entered my bedroom. I felt totally helpless. I knew I was completely unable to escape from this situation; I could not scream for no one would hear me, and I could not fight against Marco.

I heard a noise behind me. Turning, I was horrified to see Marco coming towards me with nothing on. I had never seen a man totally naked – not even my father. The next moment he was on top of me, ripping at my clothes, his body weight pinning me under him. My sobs were drowned out by his groaning.

Then, I felt a sudden surge of strength and I managed to push him off me. Marco sprawled across the floor. As he did so, I got up, and I ran towards the bathroom.

Inside, I bolted the door and turned to see a window above the sink. It was slightly open, so I shut and locked it. I could hear him start to shout. Time after time, he kicked and punched the door, calling me all the names under the sun. I could feel the wall vibrate through the intensity of his punches.

I was frightened for my life. How could I keep this door shut? My strength would surely soon give out. And then, I suddenly saw in my mind's eye, a little red book. My Bible, the New Testament given to me when I was a child . . . hadn't I read somewhere in that book, that if I really called out to God, he would save me? The words of the Lord's Prayer came to me and I began to recite it, very loudly, in between frantic words and sobs.

'OK, God, if you're really there, I really need you – oh God, I really need your help! Please help me to keep this door shut! Give me strength . . . oh, our Father, who art in heaven, hallowed be thy name . . . '

My heart was still thumping in my chest, but the thumping on the door finally stopped. Everything went quiet.

After the longest and most intense moments of my life, I found the courage to slowly open the bathroom door. Marco had gone.

Crying and trembling, I came out of the bathroom. My sobs becoming more and more laboured, as I tried to breathe. Then another fear rose up inside me as I wondered if he was hiding somewhere in the house, just waiting for me to try to get out. Now, the silence became terrifying. I strained to hear doors or floorboards creaking, any tell-tale sign that he was still in the house, but none came.

Maybe my prayer had worked. But I was not going to wait around to find out. I could see the front door from the top of the stairs and knew that if I made it out, then I would be safe; after all, *someone* had to live in one of the neighbouring houses. Through the panic, I prepared myself as I did when I was running a race. Then with one more spurt of courage, I raced down the stairs and fled the house, only checking to see if he was behind me once I was in plain view of neighbouring houses.

I continued running until my strength gave out and I was sure that he was not following me. Then I collapsed. Slumped in a gutter, I sobbed and sobbed. My clothes were ripped and big bruises were developing where Marco had pinned me down. I hugged myself as the reality of what had happened hit me. The smell of his aftershave was still on my torn clothes and it was as if I could still feel his body on top of me – I would feel that sensation for a long time afterwards.

Gripped by my anguish, I was unaware of a woman walking towards me. She was pushing a pram.

'Oh! What on earth has happened to you?' she said, kindly, and bent down towards me.

I immediately backed away. I did not want her touching me. At that moment, I never wanted anyone touching me ever again.

'He – he – ' I could not manage to get any other words out, and gave up trying. I let my body and my clothing tell the story of what had happened. I did not know where I was geographically and I was in so much shock that I absolutely could not explain what had just occurred in any kind of rational detail.

I felt sick as the realisation of what that man had done to me began to sink in. All I could do was sit there on the grubby pavement and sob.

'You can't sit here like this! I must get you to a doctor,' said the woman. 'Come on. Come with me – come back to my house and we'll get you sorted out.'

I struggled to my feet as she held out her hand to me and together we went back to her house. My head was throbbing. I began to feel faint. I clamped my hands on to the pram for support as my legs kept giving way underneath me.

Her house was large, and very neat and tidy. Light shone all around the living room and the smell of clean washing filled the air. It reminded me of my mother's house. I guess in moments like these, you would wish for one of your parents or someone else who loved and cared about you to come running to your aid, but for me there was no one. If my father had been called, I would have got another beating; if my mother had been called, she would have sent me right back to my father. So once again, I knew I would have to cope alone. I would have to shelve this terrible ordeal, along with the rest of the awful memories of my life, in the recesses of my mind and heart. As I sat in that woman's house, I knew I would have to get to a place of living with the memory of what had just happened, just like I had learned to live with all the memories of other sordid deeds done to me in the past. After all, why should I count this one as any different?

'Could you hold the baby for me whilst I make a phone call?' asked the woman.

I took the child. But when I looked down at the tiny creature that I was holding, I was filled with dread.

'Oh no! What if I end up with one of these?'

The child started to cry, as if it sensed what I was thinking and feeling. Swiftly, the woman moved to whisk the baby away from me, apparently realising that it had been a mistake to leave him in such traumatised arms.

It wasn't long before a police car drew up outside and two police officers walked up to the house. As they came in, I looked up at them and began to cry again. Fear and panic welled up in me afresh as the realisation of the seriousness of the situation really began to dawn on me. But policemen . . . once before I had been at the mercy of men like these; they had taken me back into a situation that I was desperate to get out of. Now, here I was, years later, terrorised by the thought that they would take me back to my father in my present condition. What would he say and do when he saw my clothes all torn and marks beginning to appear all over my body, where I had been held down?

At the police station, my body was trembling from head to foot. Even my jaw trembled, making speech impossible. I was being asked so many questions but my mind felt fogged and blurred and this made it impossible for me to think clearly. Even the simplest of questions was too much for me to contend with.

'OK, Shireen, I am going to take you to the police surgeon's room,' one of the officers told me. 'He's going to examine you and collect any evidence so we can see if we can catch this man. He will ask you some very simple questions. Then once that's all over, you can go home and rest!'

Go home and rest! Little did he know.

We came to a room; everything was white. The curtain around the bed was white. The sheets were white. The tiles on the wall were white. Even the desk; nothing escaped the clinical palette. I looked over at the trolley beside the bed and my gaze was held by the variety of instruments carefully laid out on the white linen cloth. The complicated shapes led me to the conclusion that they could inflict fatal wounds . . . I turned to look at the man coming towards me. My mind became unravelled as I realised that those instruments were going to be used on me. In sheer terror, with nowhere to run, I had to quickly devise a plan. Why did all the men who entered my life think that they could just abuse me this way? No way was I about to let anyone else near me! There had to be a way out of this mess. If they called my father and told him what had happened, I would be practically beaten up. I could not afford to let my father see me like this. I could not afford to let this police surgeon touch me and then ask me all sorts of questions before he, or one of his colleagues, put me in the back of a police car and drove me back – like they had so many years earlier.

I opened my mouth and words came out in a stream.

'Nothing happened. I lied. I tore my clothes. No one touched me. No one raped me.'

The police surgeon was startled by my outburst. 'I beg your pardon?'

'Nothing happened!' I repeated. 'It's all a terrible mistake!'

'What do you mean, nothing happened? I have been told that you were raped! Were you, or weren't you?' He sounded impatient.

'No, I wasn't. I wasn't raped,' I mumbled.

The police surgeon turned away and left the room. I could hear discussions going on behind the door and instinctively knew that they were about me. But the damage had been done. I had denied what had happened. I knew they would all be angry with me, but I also knew that if any of this reached my father, my fate would have been far worse than anything they could imagine.

I was reprimanded for wasting police time and my mother, whose name I gave as my next of kin, was called to pick me up.

I didn't say a word to my mother during the journey to my house; we travelled in silence. She did not believe that anything had happened to me, and somewhere in my head and my heart, I did not want her to know that anything had happened. If she'd believed it had, she might pursue the incident, and that would have meant my father would get involved. He was the one person in this world that I definitely did not want to know about the rape.

In a sense, I felt like I had betrayed my father. Although he had not touched me for a very long time, I knew that the only time that he had been nice to me was when he wanted something. If he'd found out that another man had been with me, he might have become even more hateful towards me, which frightened me even more. No; it would be far easier for me to contend with the anger of these other men – and my mother – for an instant, than to live with the anger of my father.

That night, exhausted from all that had happened, I took a red hot bath and began to peel the skin from my arms and legs with my nails, leaving long red open wounds that bled and throbbed for hours. I lay on my bed drifting in and out of sleep, with only one thought in my mind:

'God, if you are really up there, what have I ever done to you that you should hate me so much?'

Chapter 14

Romance

To my great excitement, I received a letter saying that I had been accepted into Croydon Technical College to do a nursing course. But my excitement was soon deflated when I showed the letter to my father. He ripped it up, saying that I would not be able to do it because we were leaving Croydon – and moving to Whitton in Middlesex.

That was the first I had heard about the move. There was no discussion; no asking me what I thought about a move – just a short, plain statement of fact: 'You're going. There's no debate.'

If possible, I hated my father all the more and I sincerely wanted to be rid of him for ever. In fact, the hatred extended to every man on the face of the earth – except my brother, of course, and those kind relatives so far away.

But I resolved that at the very first opportunity, I was going to be gone; nobody, not even my father, was going to stop me. He had shaped my past but I was not going to allow him to shape my future. From the day he ripped up that letter, I had a new determination in my heart to get away and live my own life.

I was filled with a mixture of feelings as I shut the front door of my nan's house for the final time. In a way, to me she was still in that house. I had said goodbye to the old typewriter, which lay discarded on the floor of the back bedroom. Tears pricked my eyelids as I remembered being that small child who played on the floor, sitting on the rug and having 'picnics' when the weather was too bad to sit in the garden. But I was also glad to be leaving, because the happy memories of Nan were all but completely replaced by the lasting visions of the torment that my brother and I had suffered in that house at the hands of our father and stepmother.

The door of the house shut behind me for the very last time. I thought about the times that I had been forcibly taken back there as a child. Now, I was leaving forever, and I wasn't a child any more. I was a woman!

Our new house was in fact a bungalow. It felt strange having a bedroom at ground level. I had never been in a bungalow before and I did not like the feeling of vulnerability that came over me when I realised that my father's bedroom was right next door to mine. I quickly learned to prop a chair up against the door handle each night before I went to sleep; that made me feel a little safer, at least. I smiled as I looked at my nan's dressing table, which I had insisted come with me. My father had thrown everything else of Nan's away; it had all been discarded as rubbish. I was not going to let him destroy that dressing table too. It had been mine since her death. I placed a little Swiss chalet which Nan had given me in the centre of it; it reminded me of Nan singing songs from *The Sound of Music*. My mother had at one time told me that I got my love of singing from my nan, which made me feel that at least some part of my nan was living on, in me.

To people with schizophrenia routine is very important and Margo had not adapted to the change in location very well. She was becoming increasingly agitated. Because her surroundings were no longer familiar to her, she was reacting very badly to the move. She started to drink more and more. It was unbearable to be around her as her mood swings went from dull to violent within thirty seconds. Day after day she lay in bed, not bathing or getting dressed. Normal teenagers would have their music on very loudly, but Shaun and I had to keep things quiet or Margo would scream at us as though we were still eight years old.

One day I decided to visit the local careers office and look at the jobs and opportunities on offer within the Richmond area. To my sheer delight, within a few weeks, I got a job in a large department store as a trainee office junior. My manager, Mrs O'Donnell, was a lovely lady. She was big built with white hair and had a kind, matronly manner – almost motherly. We got on really well and she took me under her wing right from the start. I think I was her rough diamond, which she had determined to hone and polish so that I would become a 'fine young lady'.

'Shireen, we do not have newspapers of such low repute in this office, kindly bin it!' she said as I walked into the office one day brandishing my daily newspaper. 'Please remember that we are part of a very important chain of stores. Even Her Majesty's relatives visit our establishment from time to time. How would it look if Her Majesty herself walked in and the first thing she was to see was *that*?' She looked in disgust at the red-top tabloid in my hand, before taking it and launching it into the bin.

'I wish she would speak bloomin' English properly!' I said to Jackie, my new work colleague, as I watched Mrs O'Donnell fade out of sight.

Jackie was the most beautiful person I had ever seen. Everything about her was long: her flowing blonde hair, eye lashes that met the top of her immaculately plucked eyebrows, and legs that stretched for miles. We both worked the switchboard and covered for each other in the office. She was about twelve years older than I was and very well versed in life. Jackie and I hit it off well. She gave me lots of advice about working in the office. When I started my job, she took me on a guided tour of the building, telling me which departments were on which floors. I loved getting up in the morning and getting ready to face a new day at work.

My manager referred to me as a 'float' because I floated in and out of different departments. Each day held a new challenge. Some days, I would be asked to help out in the staff canteen, dishing up chips to hungry staff members; other days, I could be putting hosiery onto a mannequin's foot. No two days were the same. I loved it.

Mrs O'Donnell called me into her office at the end of the first week. My heart was racing with fear as I walked towards her office.

She can't be sacking me already, can she? I haven't done anything wrong, I thought as I knocked timidly on her door.

'Come in!' she shouted. She smiled as she saw me. 'Ah, Shireen . . . what's the matter? Oh, my dear, don't look so worried. I just wanted to give you this and say well done. It's been a very good week's work. You have earned this!' And she handed me a small brown envelope.

I opened it up and inside was folded up money and some coins, with a piece of paper wrapped around it. I counted the money. Exactly twenty-nine pounds and fifty pence! That was my first week's wages. I smiled all the way home on the bus, as proud as anything.

'Well, it's Friday, isn't it?' My father said as I came through the door

He'd caught me by surprise. Before I could stop him, he'd taken my bag from my shoulder and tipped the contents onto the floor. I stood there, stunned, as I watched the contents spill out. He bent down and picked up the brown envelope.

'Right,' he said, 'first thing to remember is that you now have to pay housekeeping, and every Friday I want my money on the table, OK?'

He took twenty pounds and left me the nine pounds fifty pence to pay for my necessities. I went into my bedroom and sat on the end of my bed, distraught. How was I to escape from this man if I could not save any money? I felt defeated again. My surroundings might have changed but my circumstances were still the same. Then I gave myself a stern talking to and told myself not to give up at the first hurdle. Getting away from my father and Margo would not be easy and I had to be focused to figure out another plan of escape. This was no time to be double-minded. I had to be sharp. I was going to have to be one step ahead of him, but how?

Weeks turned into months and soon my life was well established. At work I felt free. Home felt a million miles away – and that was how I liked it. I could be a person in my own right at work, not a housekeeper or mother, but me, and I loved every minute of my new-found (if somewhat restricted) freedom. I had made very good friends with some of the girls at work; they were fun loving and good to be around, and they seemed to like me for who I was. They never asked me about my life, but I enjoyed being a part of theirs. With them, I remembered how to really laugh . . . and laugh . . . and laugh.

But my father was still there, in the background. Week after week, my father had been giving me his bank book so that I could put my money in his account. I watched as his savings built up with my hard-earned money. I had learned to be careful with the nine pounds fifty pence that was left to me. My bus fare was thirty-three pence and my cigarettes were one pound fifty, leaving just enough for a daily newspaper and my meals at work. My new friends would ask me to go out with them in the evenings, and as our friendship grew, it was harder and harder to say 'no' to them. But I knew that my father would never allow me to go to nightclubs or pubs. Still, I was not going to be deterred. I was completely focused on getting away from him, permanently. It was my goal in life. So, however much fun I had at work, I was never totally free. That sinister shadow of my father and home was still there, haunting me. I tried with all my might to block it out altogether while I was working, but had no success. My mind was fixed on one thought: 'Nearly seventeen; only one more year, and he can't touch me!' It was my mission statement. I recited it to myself every morning, as I looked in the mirror.

I had now been working in the department store for eighteen months. Then one day Mrs O'Donnell called me into her office.

'Shireen, I have something for you. It's your tax rebate. You've got an extra one hundred and eighty pounds in your wage packet this week. I want you to go straight down to the bank and open an account, and then I want you to put this money into it.'

She handed me my pay packet, and spoke again, with warm concern.

'I don't want you going home tonight with so much money on your person. Run along and do that now, my dear!'

I had never seen one hundred and eighty pounds before, let alone touched it. Now, I was holding such a sum in my own hands and it was mine. I looked inside the brown envelope and there were all different coloured notes and coins. I was ecstatic. I walked to the bank very slowly, thinking about all that I was going to do with it. At last, I would be able to begin to seriously save up to move out. I would keep the money safe and sound and then add to it, when I was able. At long last I could see that getting out of my house and leaving my father really could become a possibility.

I went home that evening, totally forgetting that it was Friday and my father would want to see my wage packet. My excitement was such that I didn't even feel afraid as I walked into the house and went to my bedroom. It wasn't long before my father appeared in the doorway.

'It's Friday,' said my father. 'Where's your wage packet?'

I had to think quickly. 'Oh, I left it at work by mistake. I'll bring it home on Monday!' I lied.

He was just about to leave the bedroom when he saw my bag on the floor beside the bed. He bent down and picked it up, as he usually did, and spilled the contents all over the floor. Of course, there lay my wage packet.

'Oh, left it at work, did you?' He looked at me, his eyes full of anger. 'It says here that you had a tax rebate this week. Where's the money?' His hand caught my arm in his vice-like grip.

I found it hard to speak through the pain, but I knew I had to tell him the truth. 'My manager told me to put it into my own bank account! She didn't want me to carry all that money home with me! She thought I wouldn't be *safe*!'

He loosened his grip and turned away from me, then just when I thought I was going to get away with it, he spun round and his fist hit my jaw. I fell to the floor, only to catch his hand across my face again as I turned.

'You little . . . ! That money belongs to me. I want you to go down to the . . . bank tomorrow and put that money in my account. Do you hear me?' he shouted.

I sat on the floor, leaning against my bed, a crumpled heap. My eyes bulged in their sockets, and there was a terrible din in my head. I nestled my head on the side of the bed, trying to ease the pain. I waited till he was out of the room before I let out my anger and frustration. I pummelled the pillow, imagining that it was his face. Once again, he had won; once again, I had lost. At that point I felt as if things were never ever going to change.

I never told Mrs O'Donnell what had happened to that money and I hoped that she would never ask me, because I respected her too much to lie to her. And then, something happened: something that I could never have expected.

Jackie (who was the world's best expert on affairs of the heart simply because she had read every woman's magazine that had ever been printed), began to make pointed comments about a certain young man who seemed to be taking an interest in me. His name was Michael.

I had noticed Michael. I thought he was a very handsome young man. His hair was blond and wavy. He constantly wore a navy blue boiler suit, because he worked in the store as an electrician. I soon found myself looking out for that boiler suit, every time I went onto the shop floor. I used to look near the lifts or escalators, anywhere where they might be in need of an electrician. I made every excuse I could think of to go down onto the shop floor. I was always volunteering to take memorandums and letters to different departments whenever the need arose, just so that I could see Michael.

Everybody was enjoying this. The girls would tease me in the canteen at break times, and then Jackie would make remarks about it in the office. I was beginning to get very self-conscious with the attention, whilst liking it at the same time.

It was my job to type out the letters to customers who had bought coats during the day, advising them to insure expensive items for set amounts of money. Then I had to arrange for the garments to be sent to their homes, by taxi. One day, I went down to the right department to collect a coat for delivery, when I bumped into one of the other electricians. He worked alongside Michael.

'Shireen, I wanted to speak to you. Michael is very interested in seeing you. Can you tell me if you are interested in seeing him?' he asked.

At first I thought it was some sort of joke so I just smiled and walked away. But he followed me and asked me the same question again.

'What do you mean, he wants to see me? Do you mean he likes me? If he wants to see me, why doesn't Michael ask me himself?' I told him, feeling very embarrassed.

'He's very shy, and hasn't done this sort of thing before!'

'Well,' I said, boldly, 'please tell Michael that I would love to meet with him!'

The next day, I was in the staff canteen with my friends. I was so engrossed in conversation that I did not notice a blue boiler suit arrive. I didn't realise that the person who had put his tray on the table beside me was Michael. The others went quiet and one of the girl's mouths gaped open.

'Do you mind me sitting here?' said Michael.

I smiled on the outside, whilst my stomach did somersaults.

'Er – no. I mean, that's all right . . . it's Michael, isn't it?'

'My name's Mick, not Michael,' he said. 'Only my mother calls me Michael and that's when I've done something wrong.' And he grinned.

From that moment on, I called him Mick. We met each lunch time and he would take me out to different places in Richmond. As I was only sixteen, I could not go to the pub with him and the other electricians for a lunch-time drink and he never offered to take me, so we spent most of our time elsewhere. During our coffee breaks, he would come and sit with me and my friends, but rarely join in our conversations. He was very quiet, just sitting there, quietly listening to what we had to say. When Mick and I came back from having lunch in other places, he would hold the door open for me; when we were out together, he would pull out chairs for me to sit on. He was the perfect gentleman.

He had his own motorbike, so he could travel anywhere and meet any amount of girls and he was *so* good-looking. I could not understand what he saw in me, and the more that our relationship grew, the harder it became for me. I liked being with him, but my mind constantly flashed back to the time when I would sit with Marco in the park. I knew that I couldn't go through that again, and so now a new battle was raging inside of me. The more I saw of Mick, the more I wanted to be with him and yet, I was afraid. It was as if I was being pulled in two directions and the nasty little voice in my head warned me not to trust this man.

'You know that your father will never allow you to be with him . . . remember Marco? This man's just the same. You know what he wants you for.'

I would grit my teeth, clench my fists over my ears to drown out that voice and then try to move on. Some days I could drown the voice out, but other days I was not as successful. Despite this, I got to know Mick and I did begin to trust him.

Mick and I had a secret rendezvous. He would wait for me on his motorbike, at the corner of the local park, outside a telephone kiosk.

Then one day, as we were about to ride off together, he asked the dreaded question.

'When am I going to meet your family?'

'Oh, there's nobody to meet really, you won't like my father, even I don't . . . and as for my stepmother, you definitely won't like her,' I said, calling Margo a rude name that made him laugh.

He was a man of few words but he had a sensitivity that I was attracted to. He knew that I did not want to pursue this topic of conversation, so he began to talk about something else.

'What do you think of my bike, then?' he asked me, proudly.

I watched him rev the throttle on the handlebars. I had a go. Unfortunately, I revved it too hard and the bike nearly shot out from underneath him.

'Do you ride to work on it?' I said.

'Yes, much to my mother's disgust. She hates it!'

'Why don't you give it away if she hates it so much?'

'No way!' he exclaimed. 'Whose side are you on?'

'Sorry,' I said, 'I just thought that if your mum doesn't like it, you'd want to please her.'

'You don't know much about mums, do you?' he said, with a laugh.

Little did he know it, but his words cut like a knife.

Chapter 15

Meet the Family

In some respects, my life seemed to be settling down but my brother was becoming a cause for concern. He was getting more and more violent. He had so much pent-up anger inside of him and he couldn't keep out of trouble.

As a child, Shaun had always feared my father but that fear was disappearing as he got older and stronger. So I was being faced with three hostile people in the house. I became increasingly scared, knowing that the day would surely come when violence of epic proportions would rise up between the three of them.

Shaun's hostility towards our stepmother was heightened by the way she seemed to thrive on telling my father about the day's events, and then watching as my father lay into him. There were times when I just wanted to shut her up because all she did was add petrol to an already blazing fire. I was beginning to suffer from frequent headaches again, because of the tension.

Shaun would get into all sorts of fights at school; in every area of his life, his anger was spilling out and I knew I was powerless to stop it. I found I could no longer pacify him like I could when he was a child.

My relationship with Mick was going from strength to strength, but people at work seemed to think that our relationship wasn't moving along as fast as it should be. Jackie kept referring to us as 'baby ducks' who needed to have water splashed on us, in order to get us to dive in to a fully-fledged relationship, instead of keeping on paddling all the time. Little did she know the secrets that prevented me from 'diving in', as she put it.

I didn't want Mick to meet my family, and I had no plans to meet his either. I wasn't very interested in 'families'. However, a plot had been hatched by the people at work. They arranged for me to pick up a sickness certificate one day from his home. I knocked on the door and his mother answered. She seemed like a very pleasant lady and had a warm smile.

'Oh, hello! You must be the young lady come to pick up my son's certificate. Come in!' she said.

I went in. Mick was sitting there looking very embarrassed.

'You must be Sheree. Mick has told us about you . . . well about three words. He's got a sore throat. He can't speak at the moment,' said his mum.

'Sheree? No, my name is Shireen!' I tried to correct her, but for some reason Mick's mum had decided that my name was Sheree and she stuck to it. I had to admit, I liked being called by that name.

I was so glad that I'd met Mick's family. I loved his parents from the very first time I met them. His dad was a lovely person. He was very sincere and he had a great sense of humour. No matter what time of day it was, he always had a smile. He loved to show me his garden and name all the plants. I enjoyed those times. I soon discovered that Mick's father was like a *real dad* – indeed, he showed me what a 'proper dad' should be and I loved him for it.

Mick's mother was a great cook and I admired that. But most of all, I loved the way that they welcomed me into their family. I was made to feel a part of everything that they did. I felt accepted.

Then, just as I feared it would, everything hit the fan. I had just come back from my afternoon tea break when Mrs O'Donnell called me into her office.

'What have I done?' I asked Jackie.

'Don't know!' she said, as she shrugged her shoulders.

I frantically went over the events of the day in my mind but I could not think what I had done wrong. I slowly walked through the door, only to see one of our store detectives with Mrs O'Donnell.

'Shireen, don't look so scared! You haven't done anything wrong. It's nothing to worry about . . .'

'What is it?' I said, anxiously, looking at the store detective.

'Your brother is in custody over at Richmond Police Station. He has given your name as his next of kin, but as you are under eighteen, we will have to contact someone other than yourself,' said Mrs O'Donnell. She could see I was upset. She came and put her arm around my shoulder. 'Do you want to go and see him?'

The store detective led me past Jackie, who was looking quite scared. As we travelled to Richmond Police Station, I wondered what Shaun had done.

He was sitting in the cells. I cried, seeing him behind bars. It was my job to type out the store detective's statements from shoplifters and so I had got to know her and the Inspector at the police station quite well. He had shown me another side of the police force, and helped to drive away some of the anger that I had towards the police – anger that stemmed, of course, from my own experience in younger years.

'Hi, Shireen,' the Inspector said when he saw me. 'Don't worry. He's not going to the big boys' nick. He'll stay here and make a statement. You'll have to sit with him whilst we inform your mother and father. OK?'

'I'll give you my mother's number. If my father finds out, he'll kill him!' I said as I reached inside my bag to get my address book.

'Oh, I'm sure you're exaggerating!' said the Inspector as he glanced at the store detective and smiled.

'You don't know my father!' I muttered.

It seemed like hours before my mother came to the station. She had now moved to Sutton and although Shaun and I sometimes took the three bus journeys necessary to see her, the distance between us wasn't just geographical. The sight of her in the station caused my mind to rush back to the time when she had come to pick me up from the police station in Croydon – when I was raped.

I wanted to deal with my brother's situation myself, like I had done for so many years, but this time it was out of my hands. Mick had learned what had happened and came to the police station to give me moral support. That evening, Mick met my mother.

My stomach churned relentlessly as I watched my mother on the phone to my father. I did not know what was going on. All I knew was that Shaun was in for a big hiding and I would not be able to do anything about it.

I sat in silence, as we drove to my father's. I kept looking through the rear window, watching Mick follow us on his motorbike. I kept hoping that he would stop following us and take the next junction to his own house, but it was not to be. He pulled up beside the car and followed us to the door, where my father was waiting.

'Get inside!' my father ordered Shaun.

Shaun went in, flinching as he went past my father. Then my mother went in. My father looked at Mick.

'Who the hell are you?'

I tried to place myself between Mick and my father, fearing that in his temper my father might lash out.

'I'm Michael Osborne,' said Mick. 'I have been seeing your daughter!'

'You have, have you?' My father sneered at him. 'Well, if you want to see my daughter again, you will wait here till I finish family business!' And he grabbed my arm, dragging me inside.

I looked back at Mick, trying to gesture him to go home. This was the first time in a long, long while that I could remember seeing my mother and father in the same room together. So much of me wanted to go up to my mother and ask her what she had seen in this man, to make her marry him. All the questions that I had been storing up for so many years came flooding into my mind.

I wanted to tell them both that Shaun was in trouble because of them. I wanted to scream at them and make them see the anger that was inside both of us, but I knew that I would not have lived to see another day if I ever dared voice such sentiments. I watched as the verbal onslaught began but the voices faded out every time I thought about Mick. Was he still outside? I needed to know if Mick had gone home or if he was still at the door.

It was two o'clock in the morning before my mind would be put at ease. My mother and father had finished their 'conversation' about Shaun. My father opened the door for my mother, and to my amazement, there was Mick; he had not gone home.

'Oh, so you stayed then!' my father said.

'Yes. I wanted to know if you had any objections about my seeing your daughter.'

'I guess if you're prepared to wait this long to seek my approval, you must be serious about her. But I will not have her out at all hours, do you hear me!'

I couldn't believe it. I watched as Mick shook my father's hand in a gentleman's agreement. And then he left. I went to bed ecstatic; for once in my life, something really good had happened. My father had agreed for me to see Mick; it was all out in the open and I did not have to sneak around any more.

I found it very hard to keep my feet on the ground the next day. I saw Mick at work and could hardly contain myself. I wanted to throw myself at him. He had waited till two o'clock in the morning to see me. No one had ever done anything so amazing for me before. He met me for lunch that day but I could not eat my food; my eyes and my heart were focused on him. I was unaware of the waitress taking our order, the arrival of our meal, everything. I was even unaware when she came to take our plates away, asking if there was anything wrong with my food. I had been too focused on the man of my dreams to eat anything!

Mick came to my house that evening to pick me up for a date. He knocked at the door and my father answered.

'Oh, it's you. You can . . . off. If you think I will let my daughter out with a layabout like you, you can forget it. Forget last night. I lied. You won't be seeing her again, understand?'

I sat at my bedroom window and watched helplessly as Mick left. I wanted to scream after him, but I did not dare. All I could do was watch as my life and my happiness walked away. For a moment I just sat, shocked at what had happened. I could not understand why my father would do such a thing. How could he be so hard and callous? What was *wrong* with him?

My shock turned to rage. I got up, and turned to run out of the room but my father was standing in the doorway. I had not heard him open my bedroom door. He came at me like a bull, his eyes blazing with anger. But this time I was not frightened of him. The rage inside me gave me the courage to stand up to him.

'Do what you like but I *will* see him again! I'll be eighteen soon and you can't do a thing about it!' I was shaking with anger.

His hand came down across my face, but I turned back and looked him straight in the eye. His hand came down again, but I refused to flinch or show him that he had hurt me. I had nothing but contempt for him. I was not going to be beaten this time. I continued to look him in the eye as I got my coat on, and left the house.

Once I was out of sight, I ran. I thought I had beaten him, but as I ran, I could hear footsteps. As I turned, there he was, following me. I started to run faster, but he was quick and caught up with me. He dragged me back to the house by my hair.

Margo was at the dining table. I could see it in her eyes, she was gloating at my misfortune. I wanted to go up to her and spit in her face, to show her how much contempt I had for her, but I did not. I just went back to my room, slowly taking off my coat. I sat at my nan's dressing table and twisted the key on the music box. As the music played, I just sat, staring out of the window. Tears were rolling down my face.

Mrs O'Donnell never asked me about the police station incident, but she could see something was wrong. The smile that I tried to wear at work, along with my suit and stilettos, was getting harder to maintain. My happy façade was beginning to crack and the depression that was once well hidden began to emerge. Mick, however, remained a rock.

'We'll get together at the weekends and meet secretly, like we did before. He can't keep you prisoner forever!' he said one day, whilst we were sitting under the weeping willow tree at the local park.

And we did meet at every opportunity. I found out that there was a shorthand class taking place in the local school at seven thirty on a Thursday night. I had done well in my typing class and managed to get up to a good speed. I told my father that I needed to study shorthand too, and that the class started at five thirty; so I could go and see Mick for a couple of hours beforehand. Mick's mum even had tea on the table waiting for me when I arrived, and his father refused to let me walk home. He picked me up in his gold-coloured Ford Capri and dropped me at the end of the road, so that my father would not see.

When the lease had run out on the bungalow in Whitton, we moved to Heston, half a mile from the airport. When a plane came over the house, it cast a shadow and you could almost reach up and touch the undercarriage. The sound was deafening as we did not have double glazing. The good thing about it was that none of us needed an alarm clock; the first flight of the day was all we needed. The only thing that I liked about this place was that my bedroom was at the back of the house and my father's was at the front, with a whole landing between us, with the added bonus of a very creaky floor. Because of this I found I was able to sleep better – not well, but better.

I came home from work earlier than expected one day. As I walked down the street, I could hear screaming. Then as I got nearer, I realised that it was coming from inside our house. I quickly fumbled about in my bag for my keys. The screams were making me panic and every time I grasped the keys, I would drop them. Then, when I eventually got the front door open, I saw Margo in a fit of rage. She was banging my brother's head against the wall, time after time, shouting and swearing at him. Blood was splattering everywhere, and he was hitting her back, his arms flaying all over the place to get her off him.

'You mad bitch, I'll kill you if you don't get off me!' he yelled.

I got nearer to try and prise the two of them apart but they were locked in fierce battle.

'How dare you speak to me like that, you little . . . !' she screamed at him.

'You don't scare me anymore, you evil, sadistic cow!' he shouted, spewing out words of pent-up hatred; words he had probably been yearning to say for years and years and years.

I heard an almighty crack, as she plunged his head into the wall and a huge dent appeared. Then, a sudden rush of energy shot right through me, like it had when I had managed to throw Marco off me. Somehow, I was able to get Margo off my brother. I kept pushing and pushing her, until she ended up in the front garden. I slammed the door shut. I quickly went over to Shaun, grabbing a cloth to mop up the blood that was still pouring from the gash on his forehead.

'What on earth happened, Shaun?' I asked, hearing Margo screaming out in the front garden.

'Evil bitch started on me just because I wanted a cup of tea instead of a glass of orange. Oh, and I put a hole in the knee of my trousers. She needs locking away, crazy woman!'

'Why didn't you wait and get me to sew it up? You know what she's like. Listen to her, she's going crazy. The neighbours must think she's escaped from somewhere!' I said, turning towards the front door that was vibrating through the force of her fists. 'I had better get you cleaned up. I don't know how I'm going to get her back in the house now. Has she had her medication this afternoon?'

'Don't know, don't care. Hope she dies!' said my brother.

Margo continued to bang on the door and scream for over an hour. She had the strength of ten men when she was in one of her fits of rage. I sat on the stairs, hoping that she would run out of energy. I looked through the small window in the door to see her face, contorted with anger; then, I remembered the back door and told Shaun to run and lock that, too. It was an hour and a half before my father came home. My stomach lurched as I heard the key turn in the lock. My father entered, his gaze fixed on me. He was followed by Margo, who was almost slumped over with exhaustion and breathing heavily through her sobs.

'I'm glad you're here, she – ' I had not finished what I was going to say, when his hand came down and hit me with such force that my head rebounded off the post at the bottom of the stairs.

I had just about stopped reeling from that blow, when his fist came up again, this time into my stomach. I fell to the floor, coughing and spluttering. He had knocked the wind out of me.

'Don't you ever, *ever* do that again. I don't care what happened. You will never treat her like that again!' The words came out slowly, with controlled anger, as his face came down, almost touching mine.

'Oh God,' I said. God again! Why did he always come to mind, and why should I even bother to call out to someone who allowed all this to go on? The God of my little red book – the so-called God of love – clearly didn't care at all about me.

Chapter 16

Leaving

Mick and I hatched our plan. Every Monday, he came to the house. He turned the engine off his bike, so that Margo never heard him. Then I would lower some of my personal belongings down to him from my bedroom window. Weeks went by, and my clothes and belongings were being depleted . . . then just about everything was gone. All that remained was my nan's dressing table. I wished that there was some way that I could have lowered that down to Mick too, but in the end, I had to say 'goodbye' to it, knowing that my nan would understand. Then, one day I just didn't go back to the house. Instead, I went home with Mick. Finally – *finally* – I had escaped. I was going to live with Mick's parents.

Almost immediately, I referred to Mick's parents quite naturally as 'Mum and Dad'. To be in their house and to be a part of their family was a dream. I would help Mum put the washing on the line and prepare meals, whilst Mick was down the pub with his father. For the first time in my life, I was sitting at a table, eating home-cooked meals. I loved being with Mick and his parents; it felt as if I belonged there. They had a table with four chairs in their kitchen and I took up the fourth chair.

Mick's mum would sit and tell me stories about her family and how they had grown up. Every now and again a pang of guilt would stab at me, as I thought of Shaun still left in that house, alone with Margo and my father. I knew the quicker I found a place of my own, the quicker I could get him out of there and he could come and live with me. I told him where I was, but I made him promise that he would never tell my father where Mick's parents lived.

Even when I had been gone from the house for over four months I still dreaded running into my father. I constantly had flashbacks of the time he had chased me down the road. My mind played tricks on me, telling me that someone was following me. When I turned around, no one would be there. The image of my father haunted me, even though I had not seen him for weeks.

After months of searching, Mick and I eventually managed to find a flat that was within our budget. It was in the heart of Twickenham. It was on the ground floor of a three-storey Georgian terrace house that was divided into three flats. It was a dark and dingy place with chocolate-brown walls and a kitchen that had been erected over a mound of earth with no real foundations. There were mushrooms growing out of the floorboards, but to me, it immediately became home. It had its own bathroom whereas most of the other flats I had seen meant sharing. The living room doubled as a bedroom. The house was owned by a Turkish Cypriot who was old and fragile but very 'on the ball' when it came to money. He used to gather up the rent from each of his three flats and then, at the end of six months, he would take it all out to Cyprus. I didn't care about the flat's shortcomings; finally, my dream had been realised. Not only was I now living in a flat I could call home, where I held the keys to my own front door, and no one was able to enter unless I said so, but I was living with Mick, the man whom I had come to trust.

Mick's mum insisted that we go to her house for Sunday dinner. It became our main meal of the week, as our budget did not stretch to seven decent meals, but only two. We had an hour and a half walk through Twickenham, but it was worth every step. Mick and his father would meet their friends at the pub, whilst his mum and I set the table for dinner and then set to work preparing the food. His mum's whole life revolved around her family; she cooked and cleaned and prepared meals, simply because she loved doing it. These were chores that I had hated, but when I saw them carried out because of love, even putting the washing out and vacuuming took on a brand new meaning for me. Mick's mum introduced me to a new way of looking at housework so that it became a pleasure and not a fear-filled task.

After the family meal, Mick and his father would settle down for the afternoon, snoozing in front of the television, whilst Mum and I sat together, looking through the newspapers to see what was happening in the world. Then around five thirty, she would lay out the tea table. It was always heaving with home-made cakes and sausage rolls. So, for Mick's mum, cooking and baking cakes were about love – what an eye-opener that was for me.

What an enjoyable time that was. I was able to spend more time with Mick's dad. I would watch him carefully prune his roses and follow him into his greenhouse to gently prick out seedlings and put them into their tiny pots. He would talk me through the whole process. Each little task was a labour of love. I watched him, and I studied him, and there was nothing about him that reminded me of my father. He was safe to be around. He had never asked about what was happening when I'd lived with my father, but through our conversations together and the enormous magnitude of my debilitating headaches, I think he knew that something was terribly wrong.

As happy as I was in my new life, there was always the thought that my father was still out there somewhere. It was like an oppressive cloud continually hanging over my head in the shape of my father. There was never a day when I did not think about him. Every time I turned the corner of a street, or waited at a bus stop, the potential hazard of bumping into him was always there. His voice and his face lingered in my mind. The memory of him accompanied me everywhere, every day. I religiously counted the days to my eighteenth birthday; then, he would not officially be able to touch me. The only person who mattered in that house was Shaun. I thought about him constantly. I wondered how he was doing, being with our father on his own. I hoped that one day he would forgive me for leaving him. I could never tell him the real reason why I had left. I had always tried to protect him but until I was able, financially, to support him, I could not bring him to live with us. Instead, I tried to see him as much as I could, and always made him promise, every time he left, *never* to give our father my new address.

Christmas with Mick's family was the best I'd ever had. Mick's mum, his sister and I prepared the vegetables, whilst Mick, his brother-in-law and dad took their usual trip to the pub. I helped Mick's mum decorate the table and light the candles. Mick and his family always stood up for the National Anthem and the Queen's speech – and he insisted on wearing a suit for the day, as did all the men.

I did not need Christmas presents; my first Christmas with them was the only present I needed. It was a fairy-tale day; Mick's mum even put twenty pence pieces in the Christmas pudding. I thoroughly enjoyed the whole experience – eating, talking, watching Christmas television – being part of a *normal* family for the first time in my life. But I have to admit that I didn't think much about the God of Christmas – the one I'd read about so often and doubted even cared.

Despite having all of these people in my life, I still struggled. My life was exceptional on the outside, but inside, it was still not so good. Each day, I still battled. The doctor had tried to put me on Librium, but Mick tore up the prescription in front of him and hauled me out of the surgery. I knew he was right; I had seen what those drugs were doing to my stepmother and no way was I going to go down the same path as Margo.

I was having nightmares quite frequently. I would sit bolt upright in bed, catching my breath. The same dream had stayed with me for many years. I dreamt that I was falling into a deep, dark abyss. There was no solid ground underneath me, and the feeling of falling into the sea of nothing terrified me. At these times, Mick would try his best to comfort and reassure me that everything was all right and only then, distressed and confused, could I fall into his arms and drift off to sleep. But it was never a peaceful sleep. I could not remember the last time, in all my life, when I had a truly peaceful night's sleep.

One day, whilst passing through the perfumery department at work, I caught a whiff of stale perfume and my mind flashed back to the odour of my father's aftershave.

'You know he is going to come and find you, don't you?' the voice inside my head whispered.

'No he's not. Shut up, leave me alone,' I said to the voice. 'He's not here, he's not coming, he won't find me. He doesn't even know where I live any more! Go away!'

'It's easy to find out someone's address, Shireen. You can't hide for ever. Remember how he chased you down that street? He'll do it again. He'll never stop!' it went on.

I ran to the nearest toilet and bolted the door shut behind me. Sometimes I would feel physically sick and start gagging. I would stay locked inside until I had calmed down. When was this nightmare ever going to end?

One evening, shortly after my eighteenth birthday, my brother came to the house.

'Hi, sis,' he said. 'Dad sent me over with this letter for you!'

'What? What does he want?' I nervously began ripping open the envelope.

My father had written to tell me that my grandfather was going blind because of cataracts and wanted to see me one more time before he lost his sight completely.

'Why does Granddad want to see me? Surely he only needs to see Dad!' I said to Shaun.

'Sis, it's Granddad! Remember how nice he was to us? Not like the old man. He actually thinks something of us. I think we ought to go. Dad said that he'll pay for us!'

'He'll pay for *me*?'

'Yes. Two hundred pounds, sis. He's serious.'

'Oh, that's big of him.' I shook my head. 'Are you sure this isn't some kind of emotional blackmail?'

'It's not blackmail. Granddad is going blind.'

'Are *you* definitely going then?' I asked, not convinced that it was necessary for me to go. I thought it was just a ploy to get me back home.

'Yes, I'm going. Sis, it's not blackmail. Dad seemed very worried when he read the letter that his brother sent him,' replied Shaun.

'What do you think, Mick?' I asked, as I turned to face him.

'It's not up to me; you do what you want to do. If he's paying for you to go . . . well, I don't know,' he said. He obviously didn't want to commit himself.

I told Shaun to tell my father that I needed time to think about it before I made my decision.

Over the weeks I sought the advice of my friends and Mick's family and I even spoke to my mother before deciding that I would go. However, this was the very last thing that I needed; I really didn't want to see my father again. But if it was true that my grandfather was going blind and wanted to see me whilst he still could, then for my grandfather's sake, I had to go. My grandfather had been so very loving towards me.

Apprehensively, I went to see my father. I had not seen him for almost eighteen months by this time and he seemed smaller, less threatening, and not like the huge monster I remembered. He was hunched over a table by the window. All I saw was a pathetic man who had lost everything, even Margo – she had left again. He hardly acknowledged me when I approached him, but said he was glad that I had chosen to go.

'It will mean so much to your grandfather,' he said. Then he added, 'Oh and by the way, don't tell him that you have left home. It would break his heart if he found out that you had abandoned your family!'

'Abandoned my – ' I caught my breath. 'Don't worry, I won't tell him how you've treated us all these years either. Your secret is safe with me!'

The weeks preceding the trip were torture. One moment I would be positive about the whole trip, the next, I would feel very anxious. I could not tell whether I was doing the right thing, but now the tickets were bought and the plans were made. I had to get my passport renewed and go to the doctor's to have my malaria shot and get some quinine tablets. I bought clothes for the trip with what little money I had left over. I knew I would miss Mick and his family terribly.

'Whatever happens, you'll be coming back to the flat when you come home,' Mick said. 'You're over eighteen now. He can't keep you against your will. I'll come after you!'

'Promise me that you'll remember the flight number and come and pick me up from the airport in two weeks' time. Promise me!' I kept saying.

'I promise!' The words rang in my ears.

Saying goodbye to Mick was the most agonising experience. I sat in the taxi and watched his face fade out of sight and I felt numb. My life was with him and his family now and I felt strange and confused going back to a country that I had only known briefly – and yet somehow been a part of. I did not want to leave Mick and I certainly did not want to go anywhere with my father, but I felt such a sense of duty to my grandfather.

We boarded the aircraft and I looked out of the tiny porthole. I stared at the runway and then the engine roared and the wheels left the tarmac. I was on my way – to what?

Chapter 17

Suspicions

The twenty-one hour flight was a torturous experience. We were huddled together in a plane with the smell of sweat and perfume, and children crying through tiredness and boredom made sleep impossible. My mind kept drifting back to England. I was under strict instructions from my father that I was not to mention Mick at all, so I hadn't even brought a photograph of him with me. Still, his picture was stored in my mind, along with the words 'I promise'.

Eventually, the captain's message came through on the intercom to tell us that we were arriving at Karachi Airport.

The temperature outside was a blistering thirty-seven degrees, and the beige suit and cream cardigan that I had needed for the English climate soon began to stick to my body. I had been filled with a deep sense of apprehension throughout the whole of the journey but put it down to the fact that I had to spend time with my father once again.

Inside the building, we approached passport control. During the flight, my father had asked me to give him my passport so that he could show all three at once to the controller, but I declined, saying that I was perfectly able to show it myself. I clutched it tight, not allowing him to have access to it. I was suspicious. I felt that there was something not quite right about his attitude. The urgency of his tone was enough for me to be wary of him. The same suspicions rose up in my mind again as we were slowly fed in single file through the tiny kiosk. I placed my passport on the counter in front of the glass. The eyes of the officer, who was dressed in army uniform, looked me up and down, and then he placed my passport back on the counter in front of me. I had done nothing wrong and yet I felt guilty. I was so transfixed by the man that within a split second, my father whipped up my passport and put it in his pocket.

'Can I have my passport back, please?' I asked my father, once we were in his uncle's car.

'The hotel will need it. They will keep all the passports safe until we are ready to leave,' he snapped. 'Don't go on!'

My voice was shaky but I was determined to make myself clear. 'I am going to let everybody know that I am leaving in two weeks. Don't think that I won't. And don't forget Mick and his family know what flight number I am on, so they will make inquiries if I don't show up when I am supposed to!'

'You do what you like but I don't want you mentioning that boyfriend of yours whilst you're here, and I don't want you to let anyone know that you are no longer living in my house! Do you hear me?'

The hotel was attracting foreign tourists but was also a local stopping point for people travelling great distances. My father checked us into the room that we were all sharing together. Then, as he predicted, the receptionist took all three passports. My eyes followed her as she disappeared into a little office. I jumped to my feet and almost ran over to the desk, just in time to watch her put our passports in a wooden bureau. She pulled the shutter down over the little pigeon-holes, but I noticed that she did not lock it.

'Sis, I don't know why you're so jumpy,' said Shaun. 'If you've said it once, you've said it a hundred times – you're leaving in two weeks. What's wrong?'

I glanced over at my father. 'I don't trust him,' I said. 'I know that something odd is happening and I can't make out what!'

All three of us sat in the garden that evening in silence, waiting for my father's friend to arrive. He was taking us to see our grandfather. When we got there, it was my grandmother who greeted us outside the building near the market. She looked old and very frail and her hands were shaking as her bony, gnarled fingers touched my face. She planted a kiss on my forehead and spoke in Urdu and even without a translation I knew that she was pleased to see me.

She turned to speak to my father, whose sullen expression did not change even towards his mother. Carefully she climbed the crumbling stairs, which were still as decrepit as they were the last time we visited. I marvelled at the way she moved so carefully, knowing where to place her feet, as if picking a path through a minefield. I was so busy trying to make sure that I placed my feet in the same spot as she did, that I did not see my grandfather waiting at the top of the stairs. Though it was dark, he wore dark glasses, which hid his eyes. He looked straight ahead until the sound of my voice showed him in which direction to turn. Then he put his hand out to me, and I grasped hold of it. He was very old but he still had a good strong grip – like his son. He drew me towards him and kissed me gently on the forehead. My father watched in stern silence, as if angered by the affection that his parents were showing me.

My grandfather was very emotional the whole evening. Every time he heard my voice, tears would roll down from behind his dark glasses. My father had not lied, he was going blind, and I felt so sorry for him. In a sense, I lived in a world of darkness – I had limited good eyesight, but of course that wasn't the only darkness I had experienced – but my grandfather lived in a world where his loving family were all around him and yet, was entering into a life without sight. Was it better to be blind and loved, or able to see and be totally unloved?

My grandmother dutifully brought the evening meal through to the living room. She beckoned me to join her in what was her kitchen – one old oil stove. Together, we both sat on the rush mat and ate our meal. She, too, kept crying the whole evening and she kept cupping my face in her hands and kissing me on the forehead. I wondered if my father had told her that I had left home, and that was why she was crying. The communication barrier was still hard to overcome but I was determined to make sure that both my grandfather and my grandmother knew how grateful I was to them for all the love and affection they had shown me during my last stay. It had been so important to me.

The next day we went to see all my cousins. There were howls of laughter and such a joyful reunion as we went inside. Ali had become a very handsome young man. He had a moustache and was wearing a western suit which he said he wore for work.

'Shireen!' he cried. 'It is so good to see you! Did you have a good journey over? You look really beautiful!'

His sister stood behind him. She had become a shy, reserved young lady, exactly as her tradition had taught her to be. She came and hugged me so tightly she almost sucked the air from my lungs. She, too, was crying. My father's stern voice broke into the salutations, bringing everything to a halt. He spoke in Urdu and the atmosphere changed in a second; it was cold, icy, as if someone had opened a fridge door. Everyone was quiet. Shaun looked at me and I looked at him and shrugged my shoulders, not knowing what had happened. One of my relations tried to lighten the atmosphere, and within seconds everyone was laughing again, except my father.

However, the obvious tension made everyone feel ill at ease, so my uncle decided that it would be good for Ali and the others to take Shaun and me to a fair that was in the local park. I was surprised to hear western music playing in the background. The fair was exactly like the fairs in England, and the familiarity of it made me feel a bit more at ease.

'Your father says you are here to see Grandfather. But I sense a lot of hostility in him this visit. Shireen, is everything all right?' Ali said, concerned.

'Things are not good between me and father,' I told him. 'But I can't talk to you about it. I'm under strict orders!' I hoped that would put a stop to his probing questions.

'I am your cousin, Shireen,' he continued after a minute. 'And if there is anything I can do to smooth the path between your father and you, please let me do this one thing for you. You know how much I care about you, as does my father and his brothers!'

'Thank you,' I said, politely, 'but I don't think there's anything you can do.'

'My father says that your father has changed a lot since he went to England. He has very high ideas, which are different to the rest of us.'

'*High* ideas?' I repeated.

'It cannot be easy for you living over there!' he said.

I smiled to hide my feelings. He smiled back.

'I see you are wearing the sari that was bought for you on your last visit. You look lovely in that colour!' He straightened my scarf around my shoulders in a caring manner.

Again I smiled. Shaun took our younger cousins on the merry-go-round whilst we older ones watched. Ali was very protective over the younger ones. I really liked that attitude. He would never let anyone hurt his family.

'Ali, you'll make a very good husband and father when you get married!' I said.

We used all the money that we had been given and slowly strolled back to the house, eating candy floss. We could hear raised voices, but they stopped as we entered the room. My father's eyes were red with anger. I wished I knew what was wrong. The uneasiness that I had felt from the start of the trip was growing and growing.

I turned to my cousin. 'Ali, promise me something.'

'Anything,' he said.

'If there is something going on that I should know about, you will tell me, won't you?' I tried not to sound panicky but he picked up the anxiety in my voice straight away.

'Shireen,' he said, quietly, 'I know that your father is looking out for you and is here for your future, as well as seeing his father.' He put his arm around my shoulder. 'You have turned into a beautiful young lady and he wants to see you marry and settle down!'

I felt the colour drain from my face and my heart started to hammer as the real reason for our visit began to sink in. He had brought me here to marry me off! This was all a part of his culture, something that the people here accepted as their role in life. They had no choice and knew no other way because they had been brought up in a culture that was structured around marriage and families. But this was not *my* culture. I had not been raised like them and did not want to be forced to marry a man I didn't know!

'Ali,' I said, firmly, 'you know that I haven't been brought up in the same culture as you have. You will accept the wife that your parents choose for you, because that is what you know and that is how you live, it is your culture. I have been brought up in a different culture where there is freedom of choice, and Ali, I have made my choice. I have a boyfriend at home. I have moved into a flat with him and we will be married when we can afford it. I cannot get married here, this is not my home and I have not grown up with this kind of culture. I cannot accept this!' I continued to tell him everything, despite my father's instructions.

When I'd finished, he said, 'Oh, I did not know about this.' He seemed very surprised. 'You live with a man? Do you love him?'

'Yes, with all my heart, but you must promise not to tell my father that I have told you! Will you promise?'

'Of course! I will not say a word even to my own father. Your secret is safe!' he said.

'Thank you.'

I could tell that he was concerned about me by the look on his face. I was telling him things that were alien to him and he did not understand. The family structure within the eastern culture is viewed so very differently to that of the west; could Ali really keep my secret?

'It must have been very hard for you growing up, knowing you were different from the rest of the people in England,' said Ali. 'You have western blood but you have eastern blood as well. Try to view it as being unique, Shireen, because that is what you are: unique. You have the love of your family here, and you have the love of your father and mother back home, too. All around the world you are loved!'

The love of my father and my mother? I tried very hard to mask my feelings but they weren't easily hidden. Ali went on: 'I am sure your father loves you and wants the very best for you, Shireen. I know you are torn in many ways, I see the pain in your face. But you will see – you are destined for a happy and fruitful life, you are special!'

As he spoke, I felt the determination becoming even stronger to leave in two weeks' time. I had heard so many stories of people who had taken their daughters out of England in order to place them in arranged marriages abroad. No way was I going to end up like that; I wasn't going to marry a stranger – for all I knew, a man like my father, who would beat me and abuse me and think that it was all right to do it. Coming of age and having the right to choose may not mean anything here, but I was still a British citizen who had turned eighteen and in *my* culture, I had the right to choose and no one, not even my father, was going to take that right away from me.

I had spotted a British Airways office around the corner from the hotel. I made up my mind that early the next morning I would go there and speak to the people in charge. So, with that in mind, I made sure that I woke up before everybody else. Then I crept out of the room, and quietly left the building. I tiptoed along the gravel path and ran as fast as I could in the sweltering heat. It was only nine o'clock in the morning and the sun had risen to scorching temperatures already. I had visions of my father being behind me, chasing me and pulling me back to the hotel by the hair, like he had done back home. I tried to open the door to the office but it was locked; inside it seemed dark and lifeless. I slumped to the floor, gasping for air.

'You don't do a half-mile sprint in this weather!' I said to myself.

All I could do was wait and hope that nobody had missed me back at the hotel. I seemed to wait forever and then, a light flickered and men and women, all wearing blue and red uniforms, sat down at the various desks in the office. I went in as soon as the door was opened.

'Are you all right?' one of the women said.

'Yes, just a bit out of breath. I've just run down here to make inquiries!' I said.

'Inquiries about what?'

'I'm supposed to be going back to England,' I said, giving the number of the flight. 'Please, can you tell me if I am on the manifest?'

I was still gasping a bit for breath and every emotion I had experienced since arriving here had bubbled up to the surface and was captured in my voice. I fought to stay calm, trying to play down the fear, but I felt the tears pricking my eyes. The woman gave me a puzzled look as she opened a drawer and pulled out a huge ledger.

'Can you tell me your name?' she asked, not looking up.

I gave it and added, 'I am a British citizen!'

'Are you in some sort of trouble?' she said.

'My father has taken my passport. I don't think he's going to give it back to me. I want to make sure that someone will come looking for me if I miss the flight back to England!' And then I told her the whole story of why I had come out to Karachi.

'I'll tell you what,' she said, 'I'll inform the airport office that you are to be logged in on the flight and that they must inform me if you are not on it. At that point we will contact the British Embassy in Lahore, all right?'

'All right,' I said.

'What is the name of the hotel, you are staying in? Do you know?' she asked, ready to write it down.

'I don't know, but it's around the corner, a green building facing the main road.' I tried to remember everything I could about to. 'It has honeysuckle and jasmine around the door and there's a coffee shop next door with a rickshaw all lit up outside!'

'Oh yes, I know the one. Leave it with me, and don't panic. Try to stay calm, we'll get you home!' she assured me, as she led me to the door with her arm around my shoulder.

Once outside, I leaned against the door and heaved a great sigh of relief before running back to the hotel. Every ounce of energy seemed to have left my body and my legs felt like lead weights as I ran back to the hotel.

Outside, I stopped to get my breath. I made myself look neat and tidy and wiped the sweat from my face. I tried to regulate my breathing so that no one would suspect that I had been running. Then with as much calmness as I could muster, I entered the building, walking coolly through to reception. My father gave me a very grim, suspicious look as I joined him and my brother in the garden for breakfast. But he didn't make any comment so I knew I'd got away with it.

The remaining time went very slowly. I kept watching the hours tick by, sighing with relief at the end of every day. I made sure *everyone* knew when I was going back to England. I told my grandfather, cousins and uncles the date that I was going to leave. I did not want my father to keep me from going back to Twickenham, my new home. I had a job back in England; I also had a family there – Mick was there. Nothing was going to stop me from going back to Mick.

One day, my father told me that his brother Yaqub had been stationed at the barracks in Lahore and wanted desperately to see me. I remembered the look on Yaqub's face when he had returned to his unit, shortly after I had recovered from my bout of malaria. My uncle had taken extra leave to make sure that I recovered; he really cared about me. I knew that I could not deny him a visit, and so I agreed to go with my father to see him.

When we arrived at the barracks, we passed through a barrier that was guarded by army personnel. My father told me to wait in the reception area whilst he went to see where his brother was.

I waited and waited, feeling more and more uncomfortable. Then, a group of men came into the hall. They were all dressed in uniform. They stood about two feet away from me and stared. They spoke in their native language, pointing and making gestures, laughing with one another. I was shocked. Because I didn't speak any Urdu, I could not communicate with them. All I could do was glare at them and make them aware that their attentions were not welcome.

My father then returned and grabbed me by the arm.

'Come on,' he said. 'We're leaving.'

'I thought you said Yaqub was here? Where is he, then?' I asked, puzzled.

His reply was full of anger. 'I was wrong!'

I felt my chest tighten. 'Why did you really bring me here? And why were all those men staring and talking about me?'

'Let's just get out of here.'

I was trying to keep up with his footsteps as he dragged me back to the taxi. As I sat there, and looked at my father's angry face, I wondered whether I would ever discover the real reason he had taken me to that place.

I never did find out; but I had my suspicions.

Chapter 18

Escape

Finally, the evening before my departure arrived. I still hadn't got my passport back and was beginning to get very, very worried. My brother still couldn't see what all the fuss was about; after all, he was having a good time. But of course, he was a boy – he had nothing to worry about. He was a minor and male, whilst I, on the other hand, had *everything* to worry about. The episode at the army barracks had proved it to me. Although I never found out for sure, I was convinced that my father had tried to 'sell me off'.

'I must get my passport back, but how?' I asked Shaun.

'Easy, sis,' he replied. 'You know the passports are in that bureau? Well, it's not locked. All you have to do is come down in the middle of the night and get it back.'

'That's easy for you to say! It's all right for you. You're not being watched every minute!' I exclaimed.

Shaun shrugged his shoulders. Then he smiled confidently. 'Look, if you really want to get the passport back, I'll help you, OK? Wait till they're all in the garden talking this evening and go and get it then. I'll distract them with my amazing comic routine! They'll be howling with laughter – too busy to wonder where you are. All right?'

'All right,' I said, reluctantly.

So, that evening after dinner, when all the family were gathered in the garden, we put our plan into action. Everyone appeared relaxed and lethargic (except for me, of course), so it was perfect timing.

'Right,' I announced to everyone, as I stood up, 'I am going to get my suitcase packed, ready for my journey tomorrow!'

My declaration made my father glare at me but he couldn't say anything in front of the other members of his family.

I left them and quickly went and threw all my clothes together. Our balcony overlooked the gardens below, so I could hear what was going on. Shaun started to do his comic routine, and as he had so confidently predicted, everyone found it hilarious. Laughter drifted up to the balcony and I smiled to myself. My brother was growing to be as charismatic as our father. I took the laughter as a sign to make for the bureau. I crept to the top of the spiral staircase, and peered down through the banisters. Shaun had been right; they were all totally captivated by his funny antics in the garden.

I could feel the sweat forming on my brow as I began to go down the stairs. I kept as near to the wall as possible. My heart was pounding, as it always did when I was anxious. I could feel the throbbing begin in my right temple as the intensity of the situation built up in my body.

The nearer I crept to the little office behind the reception desk, the harder the pounding became. My mouth was dry and I could feel a cough rise in the back of my throat. My eyes watered as I tried to stop it. I mustn't cough. I mustn't let anyone know what I was doing.

I was there. I was by the bureau. Gently, I pulled at the shutter.

All of a sudden, I felt a great urge to pray. It occurred to me afterwards that I *always* felt the urge to pray whenever I was in deep trouble – even though my thoughts about God were at best ambiguous.

'Excuse me,' I mumbled, 'God, I don't know what you think of me but I think you can see me now and I want to ask you, please don't let this shutter make a noise. Don't let anyone come in!'

It didn't make a noise. I thought that whatever Higher Power had heard me, it had worked.

I quickly searched through every single passport. Finally, I found mine. I quickly put all the others back and silently left the office, praying again: 'Please don't let anyone see me!' Then I sneaked past the reception desk and sped up the stairs to our room.

As soon as the door was shut, I let out a gasp. I tried to fill my lungs with as much air as I could, then I collapsed on the bed, trying to ease my palpitations. I had my passport back and I had my ticket safely tucked away – everything I needed to get out of the country was in my possession once again.

I went downstairs to the garden where everyone was sitting. My father stared at me, and for a moment I thought he had seen me take the passport out of the office – but he had not. My brother was still in his showing-off mode, entertaining the family with his mimicry.

'You took your time packing!' my father grunted at me. 'You've only got a few bits to take back. Where were you?'

'I had to make sure that everything was all right with the flight as well, to see what time I needed to get a taxi back to the airport tomorrow!' I said, loudly.

My brother stopped his routine.

'You can't wait to get home, can you, sis?' he said.

'Well,' I said, looking round at my relations, 'my manager will be expecting me back at work next week. I can't take any more holiday this year!' And then I looked at my father. He glared back.

I said my goodbyes to all of our family that night and went back to the room, closely followed by my father. I had laid out my suit and cream cardigan on the bed, ready for my journey the next day. I could feel the intensity of my father's anger. I knew I wasn't safe yet and so didn't let myself fall into a false sense of security. I half-slept with my passport in my hand under the pillow, so that no one could take it during the night.

In the early hours of the morning, my father got up. I froze. But he didn't come over to me; he had to go to the bathroom. I lay very still, pretending to be asleep, as my father walked back to his bed. I was clutching the little burgundy book as tightly as my fingers would allow.

'Dear God, don't let him take it. Let him go back to bed.'

I had got this close. I was not going to lose everything now. Tomorrow, I would escape him for ever!

In the morning, I got ready to leave. My suit was on, my bags were down in the reception area and my passport was safely inside my handbag. By this time, I was elated. The time had come for me to go. I sat in the garden of the hotel for the very last time. My father did not say a word.

'Well, sis, you're off!' Shaun said.

'Yes. You'll be all right, won't you?' I asked, concerned.

I hated the thought of leaving Shaun behind, but he genuinely loved it out there and, of course, *he* had nothing to fear. He had a certain naivety about the whole situation and I found that quite refreshing in a way. He even made me doubt myself for a minute.

I looked at my father and thought: Maybe I *have* got it wrong and there was no hidden agenda on this trip. Maybe the mistrust and hatred that I've always felt towards my father has clouded my judgement about the whole thing. Maybe it really was just about seeing my grandfather one more time . . . My mind kept going over the events of the last two weeks, as if to find some evidence to substantiate my doubts. And then I remembered the business at the barracks.

Whatever my father had been up to, I had got what I wanted. I was leaving and there was nothing that he could do to stop me. I had a good breakfast and then I went through to the reception desk to book a taxi, before saying my final goodbyes.

The journey to the airport, sat in the back of the taxi with my father, was very nerve-wracking. Neither of us said a word, but I could feel him staring at me with such intensity that it was as if his eyes were piercing right through me. The heat that was rushing over me was not coming from the sun outside (although it was hot) but from the burning of his stare. I tried to distract myself by watching the scenery change.

My earlier elation had gone. It had dawned on me that he could take me somewhere and do whatever he liked to me, and at this point, no one would have been any the wiser. I began to experience feelings similar to those that I had felt when Marco had taken me to his house.

Then, I saw some of the landmarks that I had noticed when we arrived. Just to see them again filled me with relief. After what seemed like hours of driving, the airport was in sight. I got out of the taxi and as I turned, my father threw my suitcase at me, his face like thunder. I bent down to pick it up and as I did the taxi drove off, leaving me standing alone at the bottom of the steps of the airport.

Not only could I not speak the language, I could not read the writing either. My breathing became erratic. I was terrified. Nothing was familiar. The sea of faces began to close in on me as passengers arrived for their flights. It seemed as if I was being pushed from one to another. Clutching my suitcase and handbag with my passport and ticket in it, I entered the terminal. I had no idea where to go or who to speak to.

Bewildered and confused, I sat on a seat. A man with his wife and two children came and sat beside me. He tried to speak to me as he saw my obvious distress; it must have been written all over my face. I knew he was trying to be kind, but I could not understand a word he was saying. The feeling of being abandoned was not unfamiliar to me, but not being able to communicate with anyone left me with a terrifying sense of deep isolation. The cacophony of sound around me, the noise of lots of people going about their business made no difference; I was alone. Alone in a foreign land with no means of conveying my plight to anyone!

The man patted me on the back as he watched the tears now fall freely down my face. I heard something being said over the Tannoy. I assumed this was the announcement of a flight. Was that flight the one I should be on? I jumped to my feet and ran to a desk. I showed my ticket to the woman behind the counter, but she shook her head; she was speaking in Urdu, and she could not understand me. She looked at my ticket and shook her head again; she obviously had no idea what it was.

I stood in the crowded terminal, unable to move. This was it, my life was over. I would never see Mick again. There was no way that I would survive this. I could get on the wrong flight and end up anywhere in the world.

'It's not going to end like this, is it? I know that there must be a way out. I've got this far . . . ' I squeezed my eyes shut and began to pray. 'I know I must have used up all my wishes by now, but, please . . . ' I desperately wished that I was safely on the plane, heading for London. 'Please, just one more time – please help me out!'

Chapter 19

Dangerous Journey

I opened my eyes to see a young girl, about my age, standing in front of me.

'Hi,' she said, pleasantly. 'My name's Julia.'

She spoke English! I looked up to the roof of the airport and said 'Thank you' in my mind to God; that Higher Power had obviously heard me.

'I'm travelling back to England. Do you mind if I tag along with you?' asked Julia.

This really did feel like a miracle.

'I don't mind at all,' I said, 'but I have to be honest with you, I don't know where to go. Do you?'

'Yes. Come on, just follow me and we'll soon be home,' she said, smiling. I trusted her immediately. But where had she come from? My eyes kept wandering backwards and forwards, to see if she was with anyone. She didn't seem to be.

'First of all, we have to go to the right terminal,' she said, knowledgeably. 'This one is for inbound flights.'

'But if this is the wrong building, how come you were here?' I asked.

'Just follow me, we need the next building!' She took my case and led me in the right direction.

We walked through the double doors of the next building and there in front of me was the British Airways terminal. I could not believe it. If it were not for Julia I could have missed my flight and spent the day just wandering around, not realising that I'd missed it because no one would have been able to talk to me and tell me what I needed to know.

Julia placed my suitcase on the conveyor belt and I watched it go down the ramp and out of sight. My passport was checked and everything was all right. I was on my way at last.

Our flight was not leaving for another hour and a half, so we had time to chat. Julia told me that she was on her way to Edinburgh and had to take a helicopter from Heathrow. It was so good to speak to another girl of my age. I was safe, I was going home – and the trip would be all the better for having a travelling companion who knew where to go and who to speak to.

I got to the top of the steps and was about to board the plane, when I turned to take my last look at Karachi. I knew in my heart that I would never visit again.

I took my seat and glanced out of the little porthole. There were men scurrying about on the tarmac.

'Please don't let anything happen to Shaun!' I said quietly to myself, or to God.

'He'll be fine!' Julia said.

I was amazed. I had not told her anything about my brother or that I was leaving him behind in a foreign land with a man I considered a complete psycho.

We chatted together till the plane took off and then we both sat silently as the captain's voice came over the intercom.

'Ladies and gentlemen, we are ascending to thirty-two thousand feet. Unfortunately, our journey is going to take us a little bit longer today.'

Why? I wondered. I couldn't understand much of what was being announced; a lot of it was in Urdu. Apparently, there was a problem with part of the journey. We were scheduled to stop off at Abu Dhabi Airport for refuelling, but we were going to have to circle that airport till the plane got landing permission, because the Iranian army were re-grouping below. I didn't know what all that was about. I felt confused.

'I hope this does not cause you any undue worry. I will keep you posted,' said the captain's voice.

I glanced at Julia. She smiled, and I found myself relaxing.

I watched out of the porthole as our plane circled over the same mountain six or seven times, I lost count. It looked nothing more than a small mound of earth with rivulets of water running in all directions at the base of it. As we began our descent I began to see jeeps and troop carriers following one of the major roads into the surrounding desert; apparently it was the Afghanistan troops, preparing for war. From the safety of the plane I did not detect that we were in any physical danger, though I noticed that the people around me were looking out of their windows with unease. The ground came up closer and then I saw the men. They were dressed in army uniforms with green berets and carrying guns; that's when I thought that we may be in more danger than I had originally imagined, but still I felt no fear.

The runway that we landed on was not the same smooth tarmac that we had left behind in Karachi but a bumpy sandy road. It seemed like a makeshift runway; it had no proper landing lights, just oil barrels with flames coming out of them.

'Don't worry, we'll be safe!' Julia said.

We were on the ground. I watched as the troops wandered about outside. The cabin crew made no attempt to open the doors. They sat and waited. All eyes were upon them, waiting for them to give us advice or instructions.

Still, I wasn't frightened. Looking back, I can see that we could all have been in the most terrible danger, given the timing and circumstances, but I felt totally unafraid. Time went by, and everyone sat in silence as we waited to see what would happen next. Even the children did not move, possibly sensing from their parents that this would not be a good time to start acting up or causing a fuss.

Then the captain's unemotional voice broke into the silence.

'Ladies and gentlemen, we will be shortly leaving the aircraft and making our way to the aircraft hangar that you see on your right hand side. Can I please ask everyone to have their passports ready for inspection, our stay will be brief. Unfortunately, there are no toilet facilities in the hangar, so please make sure you use the aircraft facilities in the next few moments as we wait for our departure instructions. Thank you!' His voice was so cool that I was unable to detect whether or not there was anything to worry about.

The wind outside was whipping up grains of sand that headed straight for our eyes. The air was hot and dry. Julia pulled a silk scarf from her bag and gestured for me to put it around my head and over my nose and mouth. We passed two armed guards; they were standing either side of a mobile staircase, and they looked very menacing, with their rifles. Everything was covered in khaki army material: the men, the jeeps and even the hangar.

Inside the hangar were even more troops just sitting around waiting – as we were; they sat on their rolled-up knapsacks and backpacks, ready for action. Many of the other passengers seemed nervous in their presence, but maybe because of ignorance and naivety, or even because of Julia's calming words, I just wasn't scared at all.

We had been called to claim our baggage, which had been unloaded due to refuelling. Julia and I watched as the cases went round and round on the carousel. She had brought me a trolley and together we heaved my baggage onto it. She went off to check the flight details and told me that she would return as soon as she could. Once again, I was on my own; this time, I did not even know what country I was in.

Two Arabic-looking men approached me and one of them began to speak in broken English.

'I have too many bags, you help please, take one for me?' he smiled.

'I'm sorry. No, I can't!' I said, nervously.

'Please, inside presents for my family, must have them. Please help?' he asked again.

I glanced at his luggage. 'All right, I'll help you. Which one would you like me to take?'

He spoke in Arabic to the man next to him and loaded a case onto my trolley. Then, they quickly left, jabbering away in another language that I didn't understand – but didn't seem to be Urdu.

Julia came back, accompanied by a man dressed in army uniform.

'Shireen, where did you get that case? It's not yours,' she said, pointing to the man's case.

'That man over there dressed in the blue suit, he said that he had gone over the limit and needed to get his family's presents home. I'm only helping him!' I said, innocently.

The two Arabic-looking men saw me point to them and began to hurry away, with their trolley. The soldier who had come over with Julia put his hand on the arm I had rested on my trolley and with a very stern expression on his face, shook his head. I was so naïve that I did not realise the potential danger that I was placing myself in.

'I don't understand. What have I done?' I asked.

'Nothing, Shireen, don't worry. Everything will be fine!' Julia said. She turned to the soldier and began to speak rapidly in what I thought must be his native tongue because he understood everything she said. Without saying a word to me, he turned and took the bag off my trolley, then approached the man in the blue suit, who was, by now, some way off. The two Arabic men were then escorted, along with the offending case, to an office.

'What happened?' I stared at Julia. 'I don't understand. And how were you able to speak to the soldier like that?'

'That man in the blue suit wanted to use you to carry his illegal drink. He was well over the limit. They caught him just in time, thankfully!' she replied.

The soldier came back to speak to Julia and it turned out to be just as she had said – the suitcase was filled with bottles of whisky. She had saved me once again. All I could do was say 'Thank you!' but that really wasn't enough; I was so grateful to my travelling companion that just saying 'Thanks' seemed very inadequate.

We re-boarded the plane and started the second leg of our journey. Julia spoke very little, leaving me to my thoughts. I doubted whether I would ever fully realise just what I had escaped from, or the level of danger that I had been in. I was sure that I would never find out what my father had been planning for me. All I knew was that I was on my way home. I had chosen the western life with Mick and his family; they were my life now. All I wanted to do was see them again.

'I promise!' Those words had kept coming back to me time after time during my trip – those words had kept me from falling into the abyss of despair.

My time in Karachi was something that I had to put behind me. It would now be nothing more than a distant memory; a time and a place that could only be re-visited in my mind. I knew that I would never see my grandfather again, and I was sorry about that. I was equally sorry that I would never see Ali and my other cousins ever again – and my uncle Yaqub.

I tried to picture myself living the sort of life that my cousins lived, but I could not identify with it; it terrified me to think that I could be married to a man that I did not know. Actually, deep down I was even terrified of building a life with Mick, not knowing if he would abandon me the way that everyone else had; but to me, Mick was worth the gamble. He and his family had shown me huge amounts of love, in the same way that my Pakistani grandparents had; the difference was that I had grown up in the same kind of environment as Mick and his family, whereas my grandparents' outlook and culture was completely alien to a western girl like me. The familiarity of culture was important; it outweighed everything else.

We left Charles De Gaulle Airport on the last leg of our journey and were now on our way home, crossing the English Channel. I almost cheered when we reached the white cliffs of Dover. I stared at the lights coming from the houses below. They were like Christmas tree-lights, spanning the green and pleasant landscape. The sun-parched landscape of Pakistan had its beauty, but for me it could never compare to the greenery of England.

'This is my present to you!'

I heard that quite clearly, but I did not know where the voice came from. Still, it was right; I belonged here.

I gave a little shriek of delight as the wheels began to touch down on the runway at Heathrow. It was so hard for me to contain my elation. I tried to be reserved but I just could not stifle a big grin that stretched the width of my face – and I couldn't stop the tear that came to my eye. All the trials and hurdles that I had faced in the last twenty-four hours became distant memories. All the fear I had endured became as nothing, because I was safely back on English soil.

This time there were no soldiers to meet us as we made our way down the steps, no armoured vehicles scattered on the runway, just people – people who were speaking a language I understood. I could communicate with them, and the frightening sense of isolation was gone.

I was glad that I had worn my suit and cream cardigan; the temperature was very cold, with the wind blowing mercilessly. I wondered if Mick and his parents would be there to meet me; after all, the journey had taken an extra nine hours. My head was buzzing because of the sound of the engines and my hearing had become muffled.

As we got near passport control, the crowd began to thicken. People were pushing in all directions. It was hard not to get swept along. I showed my passport to the man behind the desk. He took a second glance at me, and smiled as he waved me through. I was still beaming because I was home. Impatiently I stood and watched suitcases of all descriptions roll by on the carousel. All I wanted to do was get my cases and go. On and on they rolled by until at last I recognised mine. With Julia's help, I hauled the heavy case onto the trolley and together we made our way to the exit.

People were now dispersing in all directions. My trolley was heavy; I had bought Mick's mum and dad a bottle of whisky and was watching it closely, to make sure that it did not fall and break. Then my eyes were focused on the door that led to the main terminal. It was like a marathon, and I was trying to get to the finishing line.

I was nearly there. I turned to thank Julia for all her help but I couldn't see her. She was gone.

My head spun around in all directions to see where she was. There were only a few stragglers leaving the area now, so she could not have got lost in the crowd. I searched but could not find her. I had to thank her for all that she had done for me; I felt she had saved my life. I could not let her go without showing her my appreciation.

I ran back through to the luggage area to see if I had left her behind, but there was no sign of her. I asked one of the customs officers if he had seen the girl who was travelling with me, but he said he hadn't.

I ran back to the gate to see if she had left something behind. There, I saw the stewardess who had collected the boarding passes.

'Excuse me! Have you seen the girl who was travelling with me on this flight?' I said. 'Her name is Julia!'

The stewardess looked puzzled. 'Sorry, you were the only young lady on this flight. The rest were families!' she said, as she looked through the passes.

'You're joking!' I said, stunned. 'She was sitting right beside me. She had to take a helicopter to Edinburgh, she told me!'

'I'm sorry, but you were the only young lady on the flight. Here, look through the passes yourself if you don't believe me!' She held out her hand, offering me the tickets.

I slowly walked through the Customs and Excise area and made my way to the main part of the airport. I was still feeling stunned by what the stewardess had said. Whatever had happened to Julia? I did feel very puzzled by her sudden departure – and upset that I hadn't had a chance to thank her properly.

'She must have been my guardian angel!' I said to myself, ironically.

All thoughts of Julia disappeared as I came out through the door. Mick was there, waiting as he had promised he would. His parents were there, too. I ran into Mick's arms.

'You kept your promise!' I said.

'Of course I did,' he replied.

His dad took the trolley and the four of us left the airport. My nightmare was over – or so I thought.

Chapter 20

Some Kind of Security

Cheerfully, I answered the phone, giving the name of the store.

'Good morning! How may I help you?'

'It's me!'

My heart fell to the floor as I heard my father's voice.

'I want my money. You won't get away with not paying me!' His voice sounded more menacing than ever.

I slowly placed the receiver down on the board, just in time for Jackie to come back from her break and see my shocked expression.

'What's the matter? Have you just had a bomb threat?'

My whole body felt as though it was shutting down. My legs turned to jelly. I opened my mouth but no words would come out.

Jackie rushed to get Mrs O'Donnell, who took one look at me and said, 'What on earth's wrong?'

I couldn't answer. By this time, I was feeling sick. Both Jackie and Mrs O'Donnell took me to her office, where Mrs O'Donnell made me put my head between my knees. Gradually, my senses returned and I told Mrs O'Donnell what had happened.

'He wants his money back – the money for the flight to Karachi. But he said he'd pay. I can't pay back that money! I haven't got it.'

'Don't you worry, my dear!' Mrs O'Donnell tried to console me. 'He'll soon forget about the money, you'll see. It was just a shock for you to hear his voice again. You're home now, he can't do anything!'

I watched her lips and I heard her voice, but it didn't make me feel any better; she was being very kind, but I knew my father. After all the years of physical abuse, and with the secret knowledge of how he really felt about me, I knew that he was very dangerous indeed.

Mrs O'Donnell let me go home early that night.

I sat in the flat, frightened to move. Once again, my father was imprisoning me – in my own flat this time! I had a key to my own front door and I could not use it; I was too scared to go out, because of him.

'When is he ever going to leave me alone? Where am I going to get two hundred pounds from? We can barely afford the rent on this place, let alone fork out that amount of money in one go!' I cried.

Mick was pacing up and down in anger. 'I don't care how much it is, you are not paying it on principle. He can go and get stuffed for all I care. If I have to go and sort him out, I will!'

Unsurprisingly, all my nightmares came back. I was running, once again, down the same dark tunnel that led to nowhere.

'You'll never get away from him,' whispered the voice in my mind. 'You might as well kill yourself now. It's the only way you'll get any peace!'

One morning, the darkness really closed in. My thoughts rambled on and on. I'd thought I was free of him. I had a new flat and a new life, but he was still haunting me. I slowly walked around the flat with no enthusiasm for anything. Once I was dressed, I went to the front door to pick up the mail.

I opened up the wire cage that stopped the envelopes from falling to the floor. Inside, there was a brown envelope with my name and address on it, but I did not recognise the handwriting. I took it back inside the flat before I opened it. I had had a photograph of myself specially taken for my grandfather. That photograph fell out onto the floor now in hundreds of pieces.

I picked up the pieces and placed them on the coffee table, then put them back into one whole picture. I went numb. Everything around me faded out as I focused on the photograph. I remembered how my grandmother had sat and stroked it, with tears rolling down her face. My father must have taken it from them and ripped it up.

I knew I would have to put this episode into the back of my mind, or I would cease to function altogether. I also had to block out my father's demands regarding the payment for the ticket to Karachi. Mick was adamant that we weren't going to pay, and that was that.

I took one last look at the torn pieces in front of me. I knew that I was on my own forever. There would be no turning back if things did not work out with Mick; no family to run back to. But I felt secure with Mick and doubts about my future with him didn't arise very often. I had to get on with my life.

One day, whilst I was on the switchboard at work, a call came in. It was late in the afternoon.

'Good afternoon! May I help you?' I said with the same cheerful voice that I always used.

'You won't get away. I'll hunt you down and I will stab you in some dark alley. You'll *never* get away from me!'

Moments later, the switchboard rang again, but I was too terrified to move. This time, Jackie had just returned from her coffee break. Not realising what had just happened, she picked up the receiver. I looked into her eyes as she answered the call. Instinctively I knew that it was him again. He must have thought that I had picked up the call and repeated his threat. Her eyes widened in shock, as she listened to the voice on the phone.

'It was him, wasn't it?' I whispered, trying to fight the tears.

That night, I was escorted to the bus stop by two of the store's detectives. I was the victim but I felt like the criminal; I could feel the eyes of all my colleagues staring at me as I was escorted out and marched up the street. I felt numb and so alone at that point. No one could ever really know what it felt like to have their life threatened by their own father. There could be no rejection that was worse than the rejection of a child by its own parents. All the years of hearing him say that I should have 'died at birth' had given me some sort of immunisation to his words as they were spoken over me, but nothing could have prepared me to hear them spoken with such venom and with such intensity that I believed he was capable of carrying out the threat. The blood began to go cold in my veins at the thought of him hunting me down.

After that, I tried hard to keep calm at work. People asked me questions about why I had been escorted from the premises, but I refused to answer them. I think my declining to reply only fed their already overdriven imaginations but it didn't matter to me; I continued to keep my silence.

As I came down the escalator to the ground floor of the store one afternoon, a voice came over the Tannoy.

'Would Shireen please go to the jewellery department on the ground floor? Thank you!'

What was this – more trouble? When I reached the jewellery department I saw Mick in his dark blue boiler suit. He looked increasingly uncomfortable about something; then, as I got nearer, I could see that he was actually sweating, and I realised what this was all about.

I tried not to smile, knowing what was coming, as my eyes caught sight of the red velvet box in his hand. The man who had waited so faithfully outside the door of my house till the early hours of the morning and who had helped me to escape from my father then declared that he wished to spend the rest of his life with me. With me! I could not understand why he would want to, but that was because my opinion of myself was so low that I could not believe that anyone else's could be any different.

'Shel, are you going to marry me or what?' he said.

That afternoon, I said 'yes' to him, much to the relief and excitement of all my friends and colleagues who were eager to tell me that it was about time that we got married. How could I refuse this man? He was the one who held me when the nightmares became too much for me. He had waited for me to come back from Pakistan. I was so excited that, for a while, I was able to forget the dark threatening cloud that hung over my life. But then the voice inside my head came back along with its nagging doubts.

'No one else has wanted you. Why should he want you, knowing all that has happened in your life?'

But I didn't listen. I was happy and I was determined to stay that way. Mick knew my past and he had met my father. He knew the extent of the abuse my father had put me through. He had met with my mother; nothing was a secret between us, he knew it all. Yet he still wanted to marry me! We were engaged. Could this God, whom I kept asking to help me in times of trouble, really be smiling down on me now? Or was it just coincidence?

And there was more. There had been talk about one of our stores opening up in the new town of Milton Keynes. Mick and I were approached. We were told that they needed staff who knew about the way the stores worked, and would we like to make a fresh start in a different town? It was amazing; they were offering us the chance to move to a brand new house in a different town. What could we say but 'Yes!'? The new house, costing a fraction of the price we were paying in rent for our bed-sit, was accepted on our behalf, by the store. We had no idea what it was like; it could have been in the middle of a forest for all I cared. All I knew was that this new town could really be the start of a whole new life – miles and miles away from my father. It was like a dream come true.

It was interesting, though, how many people told us that moving to Milton Keynes – 'the concrete jungle' – was unwise. None of them knew how desperate I was to get away from places where I might bump into my father. If there was a God in heaven, as my little red book suggested, then I hoped that it was him who had caused this opportunity to fall in my lap. I had finally been given a chance to have hundreds of miles of road between me and my father and I was going to jump at it, whatever the cost. I was sick and tired of living on my nerves. My headaches were running together into a constant stream of unending pain. No, I was finally daring to believe that I could live a normal life and I would not be robbed of it.

The day of our departure came. Mick and I had loaded the rented van that would take our meagre belongings, and us, to our new home. I was excited but I was also a bit scared, leaving my friends and Mick's parents behind. They had all been so good to me, and had taught me so much in the little time that I had spent with them.

Mick and I headed up the road with nothing but a second-hand bed and sideboard, plus a settee that cost me twenty pounds. I watched out of the window as the familiar winding roads became motorways and the streets became boulevards. It was September and the trees that lined every carriageway were turning the most beautiful colours of auburn and burnt sienna. This was a brand new town with brand new streets paving every road. It was nothing like the concrete jungle that had been described to me. This place was as green as the park that I remembered back in Croydon. This was my brand new beginning and I could feel the miles literally causing the tension that I had lived under for so long, to disappear. Yet it was only when I looked at the front door of my new house that I felt a sense of hope. It was tucked away in a little cul-de-sac, off a main road; it was quite secluded. I looked up at the sky and nodded in appreciation – to whom, I wasn't sure, but I nodded anyway.

'This will do nicely!' I said.

The smell of newness in each room was like a declaration from the house itself that this was now my new life. Every wall was painted white, like a blank canvas waiting for me to put my stamp of ownership on it.

But the feeling of freedom did not last long. I soon realised that mileage alone could never provide the resolution that I had hoped. The sound of my father's voice on the day that he had threatened my life kept echoing in my mind. As hard as I tried, I could not seem to get free of fear. As far as I had travelled, the fear just would not go away. I feared everything. I feared Mick leaving me in this new place, I feared losing the house that had now become my home. I could not escape from the constant anxiety. I still hated my father. I hated him for ruining my life. I hated my own thoughts; so much so, that many times I would slap the sides of my head with my own fists as my father used to do, desperately trying to erase his memory from my mind. I would create thick red ruts in my forearms as my nails scraped down the skin. I looked in the mirror every morning detesting the sight that I saw there.

Even at night, when I was lying next to Mick, it was almost as if my father was lying between us. Insecurity was at the root of all my fears – I didn't feel secure in anything or anyone, not even Mick. He was the most patient and dedicated man who tried to be as under-standing as any man could be, given the circumstances. He tried to rationalise my fears and constantly assured me that he was never going to leave. It didn't help. He might have rescued me from my external circumstances but even he could not help me escape from myself.

At night he would go up to bed, leaving me in the living room. He knew that I would wait for him to go to sleep, so that I would be spared from having to play the role of a sexual partner that night. But he never commented, he never complained. He knew where my fear stemmed from and eventually he saw that even he could not rescue me. When I did sleep with him, I was like a mannequin. In every way, he had proved his love for me and yet there was no way that I could reciprocate – I just couldn't show him how I felt, physically. From the age of thirteen I had developed patterns through necessity in the bedroom area, and even though I knew I did not need those old familiar patterns with Mick, they had become habit. I had learnt to switch off every emotion and feeling, believing it to be dirty and shameful. Try as I might, I could not treat Mick any differently from my father, or Marco. My brain would not allow me to function in any other way.

Day after day, I fought every single cloud of blackness that threatened to overwhelm my life. The positive

words that I had read so often in my little red New
Testament over the years failed to penetrate the thick
black smog. I began to harm myself with razor blades
and continued to scratch the skin off my arms and legs.
I would sit in red hot baths, trying to feel clean and good
about myself. The daily fix of physical pain only dulled
the internal struggle for a while. I knew there was no
way that I could carry on living like this; there was no
way that I wanted to. Suicide had proved unsuccessful,
harming myself provided only light relief – what was I
going to do?

I was barely surviving one day at a time, when I
found out that I was pregnant. Then another torrent of
emotions began to sweep over me. I was thrilled at the
prospect of having a baby, but I questioned my own ability to raise it. I thought of my brother; in reality, I'd been
his mother even though I'd only been a child myself. His
immature troubles, getting into fights and so on, had
escalated into prison sentences for grievous bodily harm
and then robbery. I told myself that if I had not left
Shaun in the hands of a man who was destined to bring
out the worst in him, then maybe he would have made
something of his life. I felt I had failed my brother, so
how did I know that I would not fail the baby I was
expecting? Would it be fair to inflict a mother like me on
this poor child? What if I were to fail in this new life in
Milton Keynes with Mick? Would my child grow up and
turn to a life of crime? For one brief moment I thought of
aborting the baby, but I quickly tossed the idea out. No,
however much of a failure I was, there was no way that
this child should lose its life because of me – even if it
meant giving the baby away to someone who would do
a far better job than I could.

Mick and I also spoke about marriage at this point,
but decided against it. We were still in the process of

furnishing our new home with the small amount of money that we earned. Mick's parents were marvellous and helped out more than anyone should ever have dared to hope for, but we still had to be careful with finance. I also did not want anyone to say that we only got married because a child was on the way.

I worked with robotic precision at my job, getting larger by the day. According to my work colleagues I had become quiet and reserved by then. They had noticed that I was not as excited as a woman pregnant with her first child ought to be. Although my manager was the most approachable and kind person to work for, and showed great interest in me, I never told her how I was really feeling – and eventually she stopped asking.

Then one day, a tall lady with grey hair and glasses came into the store. Apart from her height, everything about her reminded me of my nan. She spoke like Nan and she smelled of lavender, just like her. Her name was Cath and she used to come and buy her knitting wools from the store. I was still a float assistant, working in departments that were short of staff. It seemed that every time Cath came, I would be working in the haberdashery department – the very one she always visited. She seemed to like me straight away; she would speak to me as though she had known me for years. It was strange but nothing about Cath threatened me – viewing people with suspicion and naturally holding people at arm's length had become second nature to me, but somehow Cath was different. She seemed to be able to get through the huge, protective wall that I had erected around my heart. Her words seemed to be able to still the storm of anger and bitterness inside of me. When I was with her I felt calm; it was almost as if Cath had a power that went beyond any logical explanation. And just as I never felt threatened by this old lady, I also never felt judged.

I began to see her on my days off. We would have tea together and she would speak about her life. There was something about her – a kind of peacefulness – that made me very curious. Even her home seemed to be filled with this sense of peace. Peace was something that I had longed for all my life. Maybe the fact that she reminded me of my nan made me feel so warm towards her, but I also noticed that when I left her home, it was as if I was taking something of Cath away with me, something I liked very much – a deposit of her peace. An easy, accepting kind of friendship started to develop. We appeared to be knitting together as well as the cardigans that Cath was making for my unborn child.

Cath was a Christian. I'd never met one before – someone who actually believed in the person I had read about all these years – the person in that little red book of mine. She spoke quite openly about her faith in Jesus, and what impressed me most was that to Cath, Jesus wasn't just a character from a book; he wasn't just a part of a story that happened a couple of thousand years ago. To her, Jesus was here and now. He was a friend to be trusted.

For all my calling out to the God of the Bible over the years – especially when I was in real trouble – and for all my apparent 'answers to prayer', I was hard to Cath's message and very cynical inside. After all, if Jesus really was alive and loved us, like Cath said (and like I knew the Bible said) why hadn't he taken me out of my dire situation years ago? Why, if he was so full of love for us, did he allow bad things to take place and apparently watch from a distance as people suffered? I wasn't going to be taken in by Cath's words. So at first I would smile obligingly, to keep her happy, but inside rejected 'Jesus loves us' as hearsay. I was determined that Jesus would remain just a story about a man who lived two thousand years ago, nothing more. I told myself he meant nothing more to me than that, and never would.

But then, as Cath talked about him, I had a thought. If I definitely didn't believe in him, why had I looked up at the sky that day when I first saw my new house in Milton Keynes? Why had I acknowledged a presence up there? Cath's words were driving me crazy but, try as I might, I could not get away from wanting to see her. In the weeks that I had spent listening to her telling me the story of her life – which had not always been pain-free or without disappointment – I found myself beginning to soften and my interest in Jesus began to deepen.

I began to wonder what strange power was at work that had drawn together two strangers who had never known each other before meeting and casually chatting in a department store. What caused Cath to be drawn to me? And how uncanny it was that she had read the same book that I had read so often, and yet she had found answers within it that I hadn't! Cath told me she had spent her life searching for Jesus, had found him and then seen him do things in areas of her life – areas which she had believed impossible for anyone to touch. To Cath, Jesus had been tried and tested and had earned his place in her heart. She spoke about him with total love and adoration. She glowed with a peace that came purely from love and nothing else; no expectation, no performance-related agenda, just love. The other thing about her that I observed was that she was completely secure – something that I had never known.

And so, very slowly, I softened until I found that I wanted what she had and if it meant allowing her crazy sentiments into my heart, I thought, what did I have to lose? I remembered the nights in my younger days that I would read the New Testament and then throw the book against the wall in anger as I read those words of love – a love that I had never known. Then I remembered the time I had almost been struck by that cobra when I was in Pakistan – had God kept me safe? And I thought of the time when I was at Karachi Airport, lost and alone, unable to communicate with the people around me, and then, out of the blue came Julia, offering to accompany me back to England. She'd come just as I had finished praying. And she'd disappeared without a trace – almost as if she had never been there at all.

Although my unanswered questions intrigued me, I still struggled to believe that there was 'good' anywhere in this world or in any other unseen world. 'Good' was a nice thing to think about but it should never be entertained as reality – something that could happen to *me*. 'Good' was fantasy and a place to visit in my dreams when the bad became too much to bear. It wasn't real.

One day, as we sat together, Cath asked me the question I had long been expecting.

'Shireen, would you like to go to church with me?' she said, continuing to knit one, purl one.

I didn't answer her that afternoon.

Still, Cath kept on working at our friendship until she had won her place of total trust in my heart. She was never put off by my stony coldness but continued to chip away at my defences with her words of comfort and her keenness to know me better. She became someone I felt I could look on as a mother. I spoke to her about the confusion and pain that I was in and in so many ways she was able to break through with answers to my questions, always leaving that deposit of peace in my heart. That peace may have only remained for a short while, but the small bite-size chunks that I received were enough to keep me wanting more. With Cath, I had discovered a place where I could find relief from my pain, without fear of causing myself any further injury. The deep red ruts in my arms began to disappear and the long-term habit of looking in the mirror in the morning and cursing the face that looked back at me began to stop.

Another question about church arose in my mind and that was about marriage. Mick and I were discussing marriage again but Mick did not want to marry in church. He said that he could not stand before God and the congregation and make promises that he might not be able to keep. Instead of seeing it as a declaration that his love for me might not be enough, this only deepened my respect for him. He was honest; he had integrity. So we decided that when we finally did get married, it would be in a registry office. That's what we did, when my first child was five months old. And although the affair was very simple, to me it meant I had some kind of security.

Chapter 21

Crumbling Walls

I had a traumatic time when my first child was born, as I had developed pre-eclampsia. I had been in labour for twenty-nine and a half hours and spent half the following evening in shock. I was thirteen miles away from Mick, and my baby, Lisa, and I had to stay in hospital as she was only five pounds in weight.

Lisa had beautiful eyes, as she still does today, and her little tiny fingers and toes were all in perfect proportion. For the first time in my life, I felt that I had achieved something perfect. A deep sense of satisfaction swept over me as I cradled her in my arms, knowing that I had watched over something that was growing inside of me, and seen it right through to the end. I knew that somehow I would find a way of loving this child and that I would never allow anything to happen to her, as it had to me. I would never abandon her like I had been abandoned – and I would give this child all the fluffy pink things that I had seen in my sister's bedroom. Lisa would have all that I never did.

I was so glad when the day finally came when I could bring her home. I carefully carried her out to the ambulance. She was wearing the new baby shawl that Cath had knitted for her. The first few days were very hard. Not having family around me to ask questions or help with day-time care so that I could catch up on sleep meant everything was trial and error and I doubted every little thing that I did.

I struggled over the decision to let my father know that I had given birth to a little girl. After all, he had disowned me, not my children, but Mick was adamant that my father was never to know her and she was never to meet him. I felt relieved that the decision had been made for me and that I no longer had to concern myself with it.

My mother had come to the hospital to see Lisa and had brought a beautiful basket of flowers. I was filled with mixed emotions at seeing her. My mind raced back to the time that Nan had brought me home from school, telling me that my mother had a special surprise waiting for me.

I began to feel very angry as I watched my mother cooing over this new-born child and I wondered if she had ever cooed over me in that way. But I immediately pushed that thought to the back of my mind and told myself that I must be grateful that she had come all the way from Sutton to see her new grandchild.

At that time, I remembered someone saying that if a baby is not christened then it is not recognised in the sight of God. This scared me, so I spoke to the vicar of my local parish church. He was very helpful and went through the format of the service with me in great detail. Not having any idea about such things, I went to see Cath and asked her opinion.

'Shireen, Lisa is God's gift to you and is recognised by him whether you perform a christening ceremony or not. He knew her even before you knew about her! And he has plans for her, just as he has for you. Whatever you decide, he will love you both just the same!'

She went on to explain that in her church, they per-formed a 'dedication' instead of a christening. This meant that they dedicated babies back to God, promis-ing that they would bring the child up to know the stan-dards of God's Word and to know him personally. Then when that child became an adult, then he or she would have the right to accept or decline God's way for their life – it was their own choice. I decided that if God had given us freewill to choose how to live our lives, then Lisa, too, should be given the right to choose when she was old enough. And now, I felt I had reached a place where I could take another tentative step.

'Cath, I want to come to your church!' I said.

Mick was unwilling to come with me, but he encour-aged me to go wholeheartedly. So I went to church.

I wasn't sure what to expect, but to me, it did seem very strange. All these people in the church had smiles on their faces – this immediately made me feel suspi-cious. The welcome that I received reminded me of how my family had greeted me in Pakistan – like I was an accepted member of the family. But I was on my guard. During that first meeting, I enjoyed the music, but felt very wary about everything else. The man who was speaking kept walking around the room and I found it hard to understand him, but still, much to my surprise, I liked the experience of church and wanted to go again.

At this point, my hearing and eyesight were still degenerating and unfortunately the pregnancy had not helped. Even when a person stood right in front of me, I struggled to hear what was being said, and my optician told me that if my eyesight kept decreasing at the cur-rent rate, then the future looked very bleak for me. By then, I was attending a mid-week group held by the pas-tor of Cath's church, and at the end of one evening, when he asked if anyone would like prayer, I spoke up and told them about my visit to the optician and they agreed to pray for my eyesight.

There was a fish tank in the living room and without my glasses on, I could not even see any fish, let alone make out what colour they were. After the prayer, I opened my eyes and double blinked; I could see the fish and I could tell that one was different in colour from the others! That night my eyesight stabilised and further visits to the optician revealed that my eyes were no longer deteriorating. My eyesight was not perfect, but the prognosis got better and better.

Having experienced a result in this area, I took another step of faith and in my own bedroom one evening I asked their God if he would do the same for my hearing. I had got to the point where I had a constant whistling and banging in my inner ear. That evening, the noises stopped and my hearing began to improve.

I had watched them ask their God to give me things – not money or material things, but they were asking him for peace and joy for my life. But it was Cath's prayer that always stabbed like a knife in my heart. She would ask him to be Father to me, and show a father's love. Every time she asked that, I would cry. I could feel myself shutting down on the inside. I cringed at the thought of 'Father' and I feared that Cath asking him for that would cause all the good things that I had experienced to disappear – simply because he would do to me what my other father had done.

It took time and a lot of questions, but one evening, they asked me a question. Would I like Jesus to be a real part of my life? I thought, if being totally accepted by these people meant I had to do something that they required, I would do it. I was learning that having people around me was not that bad and somehow their presence in my life was beginning to drown out the voice of despair that continually assaulted my brain. So I told Jesus that I would like him to be a part of my life – but on my terms. I must be honest and say that afterwards I felt no different, but somehow, it did not matter.

Cath had developed cancer and was deteriorating in front of my eyes. She became weak and looked nothing like the Cath I had known, but she still had that air of peace about her and she was not afraid of dying. She had given her life to Jesus and was looking forward to the next part of her journey of life – going to heaven to be with the Lord she had trusted for so long. I watched her maintain her dignity and her spirit right up to the end, so much so that I could barely raise a tear for her. She knew where she was going and there was no fear in her. She belonged to Jesus, and he belonged to her. She wanted nothing more than to be with the one that she had spent her life living for. Her funeral was not a sad affair, but a joyous occasion. The only tears that were shed were because we would all miss her so much.

At this time, I was told that when someone is baptised, they become a new person. I was told that the old life is gone and a new life has come and I jumped at the prospect. I could not wait to be baptised, even though I was six weeks pregnant with my second child at the time. Somewhere within me I thought that my old life would disappear, never to be seen again. And so, I was baptised and assumed the new name of Sheree – the name Mick's mum and dad had always called me. If I was going to be living a new life, I wanted nothing of the old to remain – not even the old Persian name that had been given to me when I was born.

I soon became very involved in the church. But however much I threw myself into many of the church activities, nothing was really changing. My old life of fear and anxiety was still there. Those feelings weren't gone at all; they were still haunting my new life – the one that was supposed to be so full and abundant.

Lisa was seventeen months old when I gave birth to my second child, another beautiful little girl, whom we called Joanne. Remembering how I felt as a child, when I had peered into the cot to see the new-born sister who was later to be taken from me, I made sure that it was a special time for Lisa. I loved seeing them together. Lisa would sit her new-born sister on her lap and speak to her in baby language. When it was time to feed and change the baby, Lisa was right there, holding the bottle and giving me the nappy. I made sure that she was never excluded from anything that I did with Joanne.

I may have come through unscathed physically from this pregnancy, but emotionally, I had not. Inside, I was waiting to explode. I was physically tired but there was the constant doubt all the time about every decision I made concerning my children. It was as if something inside of me constantly undermined my every thought.

Mick had begun to work nights in order to bring home more money and was sleeping during the day, adding to the pressure because I had to make sure the children kept quiet so he could get his rest. I had begun to go back to old habits – looking in the mirror and condemning myself for not being able to cope. I repeated old curses that my father had spoken over me as a child. He had told me that I would never amount to much; I thought maybe he was right and the intensity of trying to be perfect in everything I did was just confirmation that no matter how hard I tried, he had been correct and that I would never amount to anything.

This new life that the church was promising me was just not happening. I was breaking down on the inside and felt as if I was fighting for my life, yet no one knew. I kept smiling and trying to be as happy as this bunch of

Christians seemed to be, but inside the walls that I had erected and kept intact for so many years were crumbling away, and I could do nothing about it. It seemed the more I tried to hide my pain, the more it kept coming out. And yet no one saw. I had a fabulous mask that I wore every day. It looked so immaculate that nobody was able to see that anything was wrong. Then the voice that had haunted me for so many years began to get louder and louder, but took on a new form. Instead of just crowding my mind with words of condemnation, it began to suggest things to me and along with the suggestions came a craving to carry them out. If I were out on the street, it would tell me to walk under a bus, or if in the kitchen, it would tell me to slit my wrist.

One day, I did take a knife and I held it for several minutes over my wrist, but then I could hear Lisa and Joanne crying and that saved me from trying once more to take my own life. I slumped down on the kitchen floor, and after that I knew nothing. I had had a breakdown.

Chapter 22

Light in the Darkness

Mick and the pastor of the church decided that it would be better for me to stay with the pastor and his family for a few weeks so that I could receive the help I needed. I had been put on medication that I was not allowed to administer myself.

The days that followed are not clear to me. My mind was just a jumble of hazy thoughts and memories. The medication was taking the edge off my suffering, and though my mind was not at ease, the voice that had spoken so clearly to me disappeared for a while. I was taken to another town to receive counselling and, after a while, the fog that I had lived in whilst taking the tablets, began to lift. Counselling did help a little, although my counsellor ended up in tears more often than I did. Back home, the church was good to me and the members rallied round. Some of the women actually took turns in babysitting me.

Tragically, whist recovering from the breakdown, and attempting to live as normal a life as possible for the sake of my children, my trust was betrayed again – this time by a representative of the church. This isn't something I am prepared to share here in detail; I have my reasons. Needless to say, I was totally devastated. I was led to believe that the one place where I could feel safe was in the church, and was traumatised to find that this wasn't always so. The terribly negative experience made me cynical again; I began to believe that all the talk about love and family – all the things that I had grown up to believe were just myth, and that the church had assured me were true – was as I had first thought it to be.

Still reeling with mixed emotions and suicidal thoughts, I nose-dived into deep depression. This betrayal of trust had devastated me more than any of the abuse I had suffered, because it came at the hands of people who had *told* me that they loved me. At least I could never blame my father for that; at least he had been honest enough to tell me openly what he thought, not like these people. My thoughts were bitter: I felt that Christians made out they were full of love and compassion and yet were *no different* to anything I had ever known.

I decided to leave the church. Nearly blinded by my tears, I made my way home from church for the very last time. It was then, on the last part of the journey, as I was walking across a bridge, that I heard a voice in my head. But it wasn't the horrible voice I had heard so often before. This voice was calm and kind.

'Sheree, if you will commit yourself to me, then I promise I will commit myself to you.'

I turned around but no one else was on the bridge, only me.

Time had moved on and by now, my third daughter, Gemma, had been born. She had been dedicated in the church that I had just left. She was amazingly bright and alert for her age, and so now, a mother of three, I decided I would dedicate myself to my girls and my husband. I cooked all manner of food, played all sorts of games and provided fancy birthday parties for each of my children.

Everything that I had gone without as a child, I would make sure that they had. No photographs were ever taken of me as a little girl, so I made sure that they had photographs of every single event in their lives. I sat proudly in the crowd as they performed in Christmas plays and I cheered as loudly as I could when they took part in school sports days. I wanted to be the very best for Mick and the girls.

But everything I did was only masking the sense of insecurity that was growing deeper and deeper inside. I was failing in every situation. I kept my house spotless because I wanted to be seen as a perfect homemaker. I provided a perfect service for Mick and the children. The girls looked immaculate and my husband was well-fed, but inside, I was dying. I wanted that sense of peace that had begun to develop in me whilst I was at church, before I had that negative experience and things went wrong.

One night, whilst asleep in my bed, I heard the same voice that I had heard on the bridge.

'Sheree, if you will commit yourself to me, then I will commit myself to you.'

I sat bolt upright. Mick did not stir as he normally did when I had a nightmare. Quietly, I went downstairs and turned the television on to try and occupy my thoughts, but restlessness took over and I switched it off again. I could not sleep, but kept watching the clock go round. Hour after hour went by and the voice continued to echo in my head. Out of frustration, I grabbed a Bible. It wasn't the New Testament I'd had all those years – this one had the Old Testament in it as well. It fell open at the book of Isaiah, and these words fell off the page

> . . . I will not hold My peace, And . . . I will not rest, Until her righteousness goes forth as brightness, And her salvation as a lamp that burns. (Is. 62:1, NKJV)

For weeks those words stayed with me. They gave me a sense of security and somehow I felt a sense of *belonging* coming from them. Eventually, I plucked up courage and went back to church.

This time, I was determined that no one would hurt me. I found that if I adopted the same principles of per-formance-related relationships within the church as I had developed at home, everyone would leave me alone – and more often than not they did, with the exception of a few. I helped out with the children's work and church weddings. I was involved in the singing and the drama groups. I busied myself in order to forget. Activity was now the name of the game. For years, I worked and worked, at home and in church, to be the best that ever was.

As my daughters got older, my fears evolved. I was now in fear of their relationship with their father. I began to fear leaving him with them, wondering what might happen. I would rush about making sure that he was never left alone with them – not that he would ever have harmed them. My fears were irrational, and they esca-lated beyond belief. Mick was working nights and three children required a lot of clothes; therefore, I began to work during the day. Even at work, my mind was at home with the children and their father. I could not rest, but I told no one and I shared my secrets with no one. Every Sunday, I would go to church with a bright smile on my face and deep fear in my heart. Never had I felt so alone, even in a crowd of two hundred. All the doing, all the acting, all the smiling was failing to hide the mis-ery inside.

Then one day, Jeff, my new pastor, invited me to go to a meeting. It was being held by a man called John Arnott. He was the leader of the church in Toronto where the Spirit of God was being poured out with power in what came to be known as the Father's Blessing. Jeff, like Cath, had proved himself trustworthy to me. He had put up with my coldness as she did and he never wavered. His wife Sylvie was as kind and compassionate as he was, and nothing seemed to faze them about my behaviour – even though by now I was having severe flashbacks. Jeff and Sylvie knew all about my past but still wanted to know me *now*. They, again like Cath, kept praying that God would be like a father to me and that I would experience his love and compassion.

After a lot of persuasion, I agreed to go with them and meet this man John Arnott. I got in the car and my heart was hammering inside my chest so loudly that I thought that the whole of Milton Keynes must have heard it. Why? Because John Arnott was in Croydon.

On the journey, I told myself I must have been mad to agree to come along. But by then it was too late to turn back.

When we arrived in Croydon, I went into the foyer of the church and there stood an enormous man. John Arnott! His eyes met mine and, intimidated, my immediate thought was that I would *never* have this man pray for me. The whole morning during the meeting, I sweated and fought to stay in the building. Jeff recognised the fight that was going on inside me, and he didn't leave my side.

At lunch time, we all went to a pizza restaurant. As we sat there, I looked at my fellow diners. They were all laughing and joking. I wanted to scream at them: '*Don't you realise this is where all my pain began? Don't you see how hard it is for me?*'

In an instant, I tried to run for it, but Jeff and another man who had come to the meeting stopped me and would not allow me to escape. (For which, to this day, I am most grateful.)

That afternoon, I was really panicking, fighting with myself, telling myself that John Arnott was *not* going to pray with me. No one was going to get near me. I was an impenetrable fortress, or so I thought. But then I heard that clear, calm voice – the one that I now knew was the voice of my God.

'Sheree, this man is going to pray for you!'

'No way!' I said.

John Arnott was praying for people, one by one; so was his wife, Carol. I watched as Carol came nearer and nearer to me. I backed away and stood near a pile of chairs so that I could be overlooked. Then Carol came up . . . but suddenly turned on her heel and walked in the opposite direction. I gave a huge sigh of relief, thinking it was all over. But then the still, calm voice of my Saviour said quietly:

'Sheree, I told you that this man was going to pray for you. Look down!'

I looked down. Lots of people had been prayed for and had fallen (or, as some people call it, been 'slain') in the Spirit. The heads of all the bodies of the people were lying in such a way that a perfect path had been formed connecting John Arnott and me! So, John did pray for me that afternoon. It felt like every word he spoke was piercing my darkness with bright light. And so it was that when I went home that night, it was as if I had a fresh new pair of eyes that saw things differently. Something had changed, deep inside me. All the confusion and battles that had raged within me for years were suddenly over. There was a stillness in my soul that I still cannot explain.

Afterwards, I was advised by Jeff that it would be good to visit with Dennis and Melanie, who were friends of John Arnott. They were part of a team of people who were keen to pray with me to finalise all that

God had done for me that afternoon. I did not want to lose the feelings that I had right then, but I knew Jeff was right. If I wanted to be free for ever then I had to make the effort to go the extra mile, and if Jeff was prepared to go with me, then I would do it.

But of course, it meant going back one more time . . . to Croydon.

The second journey back to Croydon filled me with even more dread than the first. God, through John Arnott, had released something into my life but things still weren't completely right in me. As we travelled through south Croydon, I saw that billboard above the bus station. *Have you ever looked at your child and wished they were dead?* And the words screamed into my soul.

Chapter 23

Shireen is Safe

I walked into the living room. There were Dennis and Melanie. My old suspicions surfaced again and I cautiously shook their hands. Still, I was here now. I *had* to trust them. I sat down and made myself as comfortable as I could.

I was asked to close my eyes. I did so. After a minute, Dennis' voice cut through the silence.

'Sheree, what do you see?'

I began to shudder. I was in a room. The room was dark and I could literally smell the fear that was in the air. I looked around and saw a shadow cowering in the corner. It was a child, wearing a white nightdress and holding a teddy-bear. She was hiding her face. There was no one else in the room with her, yet still she hid her face.

'Sheree, what else do you see?' came Dennis' voice.

Again I looked. Light accentuated the outline of the door to the room and in the light there was movement. The shadow of a man was moving closer and closer to the door. I heard the sound of heavy breathing and I could feel beads of perspiration begin to rise on my forehead. My heart began to pound as if matching the rhythm of the man's breathing. In amongst it all, I could hear the child whimpering. She was cold and alone and desperately afraid. All this I conveyed to Dennis before I opened my eyes.

'Sheree, I know that this is hard, but keep looking. I want you to see something!' Dennis said, calmly.

Obediently, I closed my eyes again and went back to that room. This time I was an adult in the room and I was talking to the child, reassuring her that she was not alone but that I was there with her. I held her hand and we both waited for the door to open. As it did, a different, brighter light shone through the door and a man stood there in a white robe. I instinctively knew who the man was. It was the same man who I had read about so often in my little red New Testament. It was Jesus. How did I know? Well, I just did. What did he look like? The only thing I remember was the kindness and compassion and how the light shone through the hole in the palm of his hand as he took the little girl's hand in his. Once he was holding her, she was at peace and the brightness of the light that shone around him radiated over her. She turned around and faced me and the smile that lit up her face told me all I needed to know – she was all right and safe to let go of. They both walked through the light and I opened my eyes.

'Sheree, it's time to let go of her and move on now!' Dennis said, softly, as he realised that I had seen what he wanted me to see.

My pulse rate came down and the beads of perspiration disappeared and suddenly I was smiling from ear to ear. I felt as though I really was free. The tormented little girl inside of me, the child who had been silently screaming for so many years, was now at peace. She had never had a voice; she had had no one to hear her cries, but now her crying was over and she had the attention of someone with whom she felt truly safe. At that moment, as I watched her go through to the light, I knew Dennis was right; I could let go. Only Jesus could know the extent of her suffering, only he could place his finger on her hurt and cause it to evaporate in a twinkling of an eye. In my heart I knew that he had cried with her each night, as she laid her head on the pillow. He had experienced everything that she had, and had not left her. He knew the very moment that she would be able to acknowledge him, to really open herself up to him, and at that right moment, he came – not one minute too early or one minute too late, but just at the very right time. She had accepted his hand of friendship and knew that she could trust him enough to go with him wherever he went.

'Sheree, there is one more thing that you must do,' Dennis said.

'What is it?' I asked, still resting in the tremendous peace I now felt.

'You need to forgive your father, mother, stepmother and the man who raped you. Once you have done that you will be free from your past!' said Dennis.

My heart hit the floor and I could feel a sickness rising up inside of me. *Forgive them!* Why *should* I forgive them? What right did they have to be let off the hook like that? I could feel the sickness turn to anger. I had hated them for so many years for what they had done to me. I was not about to forgive them now and say that it was all right for them to have done that – no way!

'Sheree, do you think that by forgiving them, you are saying that it was as if they had the right to do what they did?' Dennis asked, calmly.

I was shocked by his question, wondering if he really had the ability to read my mind. I began to cry.

'Yes I do. All those years that they stole . . . If I forgive them it will be like they have won!' I said through my tears.

'Sheree, the only one suffering here is you, and I am only concerned with you. If you forgive them and let go of them, you will be free to live your life. Nothing of your past will be able to jump up and bite you! You will have peace, you will be happy and most of all, you can start being yourself. You have lived with the image of all the roles that you were forced to play for so many years that you do not even know who you really are. And I for one want to see *you*, the real you – don't you?'

I knew in my heart he was right, but the struggle to do it was so intense. It was true; I had lived under the shadow of all the roles that I played in my father's house. For many years I blamed myself for my mother leaving. I believed that I was an evil child who had driven my mother and my baby sister away by something that I had done, even though I did not know what it was. From a young age I fought every minute of every day trying to make up to my brother for the loss that he had suffered. We were both at the mercy of a man who thought nothing of beating his children until they bled and were bruised, internally as well as externally. I took my beatings, believing them to be the appropriate punishment for the fact that he had been left with two small children to bring up – and, as he said, because of us, he had no life. From the age of nine, I had tried to step into the breach and become his housekeeper, thinking that if I made an immaculate job of the housework then his life would be better and the beatings would stop. I could never get it right and the beatings never stopped. Before I was ten I had to fill my mother's shoes in many ways. Then at the age of thirteen I filled her last role, as his wife.

I was robbed of many things, my childhood, my adolescence and my innocence. All had been stripped away from me, along with my mother, sister and my beloved nan. No one could ever replace those years and no one could really know the pain and confusion that it had left me with as an adult. I was never valued as a child and learnt never to value anything; I placed no importance on anyone. To me, no one was to be trusted; that was the only way I could function and not be hurt any more. If that was to be taken from me, how would I survive? My experiences had shaped me into the person that I was and my foundations were built on the betrayal that I had suffered. I knew no other way.

But there was one thing I was certain of – I was tired from all the struggling. The more Dennis spoke to me, the more I knew that if I was to have some quality of life, I had to let go of it all. I came to the quiet conclusion that I may never have many – or any – of my questions answered. I might never know the real reason why my father hated me so much. But in the end, I had to ask: was my life going to be ruled by this? I may never really know why my mother never came back for me when she had settled into a new house and a new life, but I was going to lose my future if I continued to look back on all these unanswered questions. I had a life to live *now* and I wanted some quality within it. If this forgiveness was the price, then I would have to do it. So I chose to forgive.

The child in me was at peace, but now Sheree the adult had to be free. Dennis had told me to write a letter to my father cataloguing all the things that he had done to me. It began in a hateful manner. I verbalised all of my anger and grief. I told him what I had lost because of him. But then, the anger subsided and something took over in me and I began to tell him what I had hoped for in a father. I told him how it hurt that he had never held me in his arms or told me that he loved me. I told him that the physical bruises that I was left with were far less painful than the words of hatred that he had spoken over me at such a young age.

And then I remembered the small child who had left that bedroom and was safe for ever in the arms of another father, Father God, who would always love and protect her. And I realised that this loving Father was the one I had always hoped for.

I went back to Croydon for one last visit to the park. I wanted to lay my past to rest and it seemed fitting that this should be the place that I did it. I took flowers to place as if on a grave. No one seeing the flowers in the park would have known that these signified the end of a chapter in someone's life – but *I* knew. As I leaned over the railings, my eyes were drawn to the hut where I had hidden with Shaun, that night when I took my first overdose. I closed my eyes and saw the little girl again, but this time she was not alone. Jesus was there, stroking her forehead. Again the light was shining over her as it did him. I felt warmth rising up inside of me, and reassurance that she was safe in his arms. I looked over to the place where the child who had turned into an adolescent and was savouring her first taste of life as an adult used to sit and read her books. It was the same place that she had been taken from before experiencing the horrors of rape.

My vision clouded and tears came as I remembered. Then, as I closed my eyes, I experienced something similar to what had happened when I was with Dennis. I saw the bathroom at Marco's house. And I saw who was in the bathroom with me, as I tried to make my escape. I saw myself praying, reciting the Lord's Prayer, asking for strength to keep the door locked. Jesus showed me that he had indeed given me the strength I had needed, and that it was he who had prompted me to leave when it was safe.

He showed me, too, that he was there when I was abandoned at Karachi Airport with no means of communication. He had sent a girl of my own age, someone he knew I would be able to relate to, in order to bring me home. He had even given me Cath because he knew that a little old lady proved no threat to me, and that I could accept the message about him and his love from her – I would not have accepted it from anyone else. A catalogue of events had been orchestrated by him in such a way that the sheer *love* cut right through the heart of my cynicism and unbelief and, in an instant, it was gone for ever. In every way Jesus had proved that he was indeed someone who could be trusted.

I opened my eyes again. This time the park looked smaller, not as imposing as it did when I was a child. It became just a park. In my mind's eye, I saw me as the little girl, sitting on a swing. She was laughing and screaming with excitement.

'Take me higher, Daddy, take me higher!'

And indeed my heavenly Father has continued to take me higher. Every day, I go to a place in my thoughts and dreams, and there he is. I continue to read my Bible where I catch further glimpses of my Father in heaven and how he feels towards me. This book, in the part of the New Testament called 1 Corinthians, says, 'Now I know in part; then I shall know fully, even as I am fully known' (1 Cor. 13:12, NIV). So I know I can't understand everything yet, but some day I *will* know in full. Until then, Jesus has given me the opportunity to live in freedom and is continually teaching me how to get the best out of life. I have chosen to live using the guidelines that he has laid down and I have found that it frees me from bitterness and fear.

In his book, anxiety has no place and anger is uprooted, leaving nothing but peace. Like many others, I used to think that God was some far off being who was up there with a big stick ready to beat me over the head whenever I – inevitably – did something wrong. But the prayer that many prayed over me has finally been answered. For now I know that God is very different from the picture that I used to have of him. Now I see him as *Father* and he understands and accepts me – just as he understood and accepted that small child Shireen, the little girl who was me. I can tell him when I am angry and feel that life is unfair. I can be honest and tell him when I think that life stinks, because he knows me better than I know myself.

I feel guilty sometimes, because of all the years that I spent believing that if he was there at all, he didn't care, or that he wanted to punish me. There were times when I even hated him, but he understands where that hatred stemmed from. He continually and faithfully keeps reminding me that I do not have to feel that guilt any more. After all, I'm his daughter; my Father loves me.

Epilogue

I've called this book *Broken Wings* because that's how I felt – like a fluttering, helpless bird that should have been able to fly and soar just like the magnificent eagle I saw and helped to feed with salt beef in Karachi. Like that bird, I'd been damaged when I was small. Someone had taken away my ability to 'fly' right at the start if my life. But just as the eagle was restored to health by the love of its owner, so I was restored by my Father who loved me.

No person could ever understand what it is like for a child who lives with the consequences of their parents' actions. No one can answer the ultimate question that lurks inside that child's mind: '*Why*?' No one could ever understand what it is like for a child to be opened up to experience feelings and sensations at a time when they are too immature and vulnerable to know how to deal with them. No one can understand what it feels like for a child to become merely a vessel that an adult will use to relieve themselves of frustration and anger. No one can understand, except Jesus.

When a child has been violated in such a damaging way, I have come to see that they cease to grow or mature from that point. Effectively their life ends at the moment that they experience such trauma, and they remain at the age they were when it happened. I know this because Jesus showed me the very hour that I stopped growing.

For many years I had struggled with a sense of not belonging. In my teenage years, I had been introduced to a world and a culture that was so far removed from the one that I had grown up in that the experience had left me with even more doubts as to who I really was. I even wondered whether my father was so hostile to me because I had shown no obvious signs that I came from his culture – was I too western for him? I don't know.

All I can tell you is this: I feel loved and secure and I live in real peace, just as my dear friend Cath did. I enjoy a loving relationship with my husband. He hasn't given his life to Jesus yet, and obviously at times this causes friction. But Mick and I have now been together for over twenty-seven years – the man who waited on the doorstep for me all those years ago is the love of my life.

These days, I invest my time in helping others realise their potential in living new and extraordinary lives with the help of the same person who released me from my dark prison of fear.

God has given me eyes to see the child within the adult; in effect, he has given me the capacity to reach those children inside who may never have been heard before. They need to express their feelings the same as an adult does; they have questions that need answers and they have pain that needs healing. The confusion that lies within an abused child is so deep and so profound that no amount of years can ever make that pain go away. An experience or a word can inflict terrible damage, and can have such repercussions in a person's life that it shapes not only who they are, but how they view the world around them.

We all need to feel we belong; we need this so we can know that each and every one of us is important and valued. But the road to wholeness is filled with pitfalls and the path can sometimes narrow to what feels like a tightrope. There have been places along my own path that have been marked with times where I have had to choose to forgive those in my past – and those in my present. I have chosen to go forward and not look back, because if I do, I can quite easily miss my footing, fall, and end up more wounded than ever. I've had my problems with church, and I know many other people have, too. But I have come to see that God *wants* his people in fellowship together. Relationships within the church family are so important; it's there that we can find love and support as we grow in our faith in Jesus, as we are helped by others who know him too.

I believe that there must come a moment in each person's life when they know there must be more than the seventy or so years we live on this earth, and much more than we can see with our natural vision. I have chosen to follow the way shown to me in God's Word, the Bible; it has become my manual for a full life. Many people choose not to follow the way of this book, because it requires diligence and perseverance and a constant letting go of wrongs that have been done to us. It's not an easy option, but if we decide to choose this way, we have a promise that we will never have to go through this life alone. We will never have to do anything that the Author of the book was unwilling to do himself. He suffered excruciating pain. He knew rejection and he knew what it was to be totally abandoned; that is how he was able to understand and come to the rescue of that little girl, Shireen, who was me.

I have become a lover of people. I love men! I talk to anyone, believing each to be precious in the sight of God. I spend time telling others where I have come from – and pointing to the one who set me free. I go into prison, I speak to the prisoners; some have committed rape, and some have even abused children. Although I can never condone what they have done, I do not allow myself to become judgemental towards them. In some respects, I understand just how they become that way. It has been said that if someone has been abused as a child, they in turn will go on to abuse their own children. I lived under that curse for many years and through the grace of God never beat or abused my children – but like I said, it was only through *his* grace that I never did.

My friend Dennis once said that I was like a closed book. With that in mind, and also because of a visit I once made to an elderly lady, I have told my story. She was a lovely lady in her mid-seventies. I was visiting her whilst hosting a Christmas party for those in sheltered housing on a nearby estate. We sat and spoke about family. I looked into her eyes that were now dull but must once have been a vibrant shade of green. She wrung her hands as she spoke. I looked around her room. No photographs of a husband or children adorned the mantelpiece. On her finger there was no sign that a wedding band had once been placed there. She was all alone, with no one to share her days with. Her story was a tragic one. She had been abused as a child and had never dared let anyone into her life since then. Her life stopped at the age of eleven. She felt that it was too risky to love anyone or allow anyone to love her. All I could do was hold her, and share her tears at a wasted life. I told her about my friend Jesus and how he had helped me. And I watched as I saw the child in her accept him; I knew it was just the right time. I believe that this lovely lady is now with him.

Survivors of sexual and physical abuse might not be able to go back to the age where their lives effectively ended and they may never recapture their youth but I know that with love, care and the support of very good friends and family, they can be restored so that they can fully enjoy what life has yet to offer them. If it were not for particular people who refused to give up on me, I know that I would not be where I am today. There are some people in this world who need others to go the extra mile for them; they need the kind of people who continually show, through their actions, the value that is placed on an individual life; a life that might have once been lived almost in invisibility. Love that was once threatening and something to be feared becomes something that we warm to and, in time, fully embrace. Being set free from the shame of all that went on and realising that we do not have to live with misplaced guilt (which can do such damage in later life) is often the liberating factor. Nightmares can become fewer and fewer until they stop altogether and sleep becomes restful, as it should be.

I can almost hear you asking: 'Sheree, have you *really* forgiven your father?' Yes, I have. But I will not pretend to you that we have loving contact; in fact I have had no contact with him since I moved away with Mick. However, my fear of him has now completely gone and I know if I ever do meet him again, I will be able to stand and not run away from him.

I have contact with my mother and sister and my brother Shaun. Shaun is now living abroad. He is a Christian and is working out his own issues with the help of our heavenly Father. My mother and sister have not committed their lives to Jesus as yet although they acknowledge what has happened in my life; it is an unspoken witness to the power of Jesus. I don't have day-to-day contact with my mother and Debbie but we do keep in touch and we now have a good relationship. The hatred that I once felt towards my mother has gone. It was only when the hatred disappeared that I could even begin to try to understand how it was for her. Many people have asked why she never came back for me. My guess is that the fear of dealing face to face with my father was too much for her and she was unable to break through that fear. I believe that it was not that she did not want my brother and me, but that it was just too difficult for her to come and try to take us.

The bottom line is that I may never fully know, and may never have all my questions answered; but now, it doesn't matter. My past no longer haunts me or shapes who I am. I am free to be the person that I was created to be, whole, complete and living in a level of security and peace that, years ago, I could only dream about. And I know that people aren't perfect; they let us down and we let them down, too. We're all just human. But God will never let us down. He's not lukewarm about us, or cold and uncaring as I once thought; he's passionate about you, and he's passionate about me.

So, I now have a new name and a new life. But best of all, I am free; my broken wings are healed and repaired and I can fly as God intended. And for that and for everything, I can freely praise him: for I *know* I am the precious and highly valued daughter of a mighty King – my loving Father God.

If you have been affected by this book and would like to contact Sheree, you can write to her at:

Sheree Osborne
c/o Authentic Media
9 Holdom Avenue
Bletchley
Milton Keynes
MK1 1QR
England

ChildLine
Tel: 0800 1111
www.childline.org.uk